beautiful
no-mow
yards

Evelyn J. Hadden

beautiful no-mow yards

50 amazing lawn alternatives

Evelyn J. Hadden

Timber Press
Portland · London

Copyright © 2012 by Evelyn J. Hadden. All rights reserved.

Frontispiece by Saxon Holt.

Published in 2012 by Timber Press, Inc.

The Haseltine Building
133 S.W. Second Avenue, Suite 450
Portland, Oregon 97204-3527
timberpress.com

2 The Quadrant
135 Salusbury Road
London NW6 6RJ
timberpress.co.uk

Printed in China

Library of Congress Cataloging-in-Publication Data

Hadden, Evelyn J.
    Beautiful no-mow yards: 50 amazing lawn alternatives/Evelyn J. Hadden.—1st ed.
        p. cm.
    Includes bibliographical references and index.
    ISBN 978-1-60469-238-9
1. Gardens–Design. 2. Ground cover plants. I. Title. II. Title: Fifty amazing lawn alternatives.
    SB473.H25 2012
    635.9′64–dc23
                                    2011020832

A catalog record for this book is also available from the British Library.

To the many fabulous, fascinating gardeners who shared their stories with me and invited me into their gardens. Not just those who made it into these pages, but every one of you. It has been an inspiration to meet you all and see (or just hear about) the magical places you have made and loved. Your connections with your gardens feed my hope for humanity.

contents

foreword

For decades, gardeners on this side of the Atlantic have emulated the vast, perfect lawns of English estate-owners, who flaunted their wealth by devoting their land to an unproductive use. We've coddled and fussed with our lawns in hopes of creating something that meets the high expectations of golfers, all too often by following the advice in ubiquitous ads telling us to "green up" our lawns with repeated applications of products. But finally we're beginning to see that we don't have to conform to that crazy standard anymore. People are starting to challenge local laws and homeowner association rules that require the growing of lawn or, even worse, that lawns be green all summer—and they're winning those challenges.

Slowly we're learning about the environmental damage done in the name of the Great American Lawn—the wasted water, the fertilizers running off into waterways, the lawn pesticides harming everything they touch: pollinators, soil, humans, and pets. We're seeing connections between disappearing wildlife and the vast acreage we've devoted to a single plant that provides virtually nothing for wildlife. And then there are those fume-spewing mowers and blowers.

I had a lawn for many years myself, but eventually all those negatives plus being bored to tears by lawn care inspired me to remove it all— *done!* Well, not so easy. To replace it with what? Researching "lawn replacement" usually yielded just one solution: a big meadow. Where were the inspiring design ideas for regular-sized yards? Or the array of plants that had proven tough and sustainable in spots that were once lawn? Or some realistic advice about how to maintain them? Despite my decades of gardening, I had no idea how to convert my lawn to something that might really work.

But in my search for alternatives I *did* find someone who'd been speaking and writing about lawn reduction for a decade already, and it was Minnesota rabble-rouser Evelyn Hadden. So I enlisted her and a few others excited about this subject, and we formed the Lawn Reform Coalition to spread the word about natural lawn care, better types of grasses, and ways to reduce or eliminate lawns altogether.

But the coalition's website (lawnreform.org) can't showcase the whole range of alternatives to the bad old ways of lawns and lawn care, with stories about real gardeners who've created gardens that are healthier and far more satisfying. To fill that void, we now have *Beautiful No-Mow Yards.* It's packed with photos (many by the renowned Saxon Holt) of real gardens, including my own, where I endured several failures in the search for effective lawn alternatives. If only this book had existed a few years ago!

In her book Evelyn has used the same inclusive approach adopted by the Lawn Reform Coalition—avoiding finger-pointing and the simplistic one-solution-for-everyone advice we find in so much information about "sustainable gardening." Instead, she gently leads readers to make peace with their land by growing plants that connect them with nature, and by creating spaces to gather, play, and calm their overworked souls.

Beautiful No-Mow Yards is an important book not just because it's so darn definitive, but because it's for such a large audience: eco-minded non-gardeners trying to reduce their lawn, beginning gardeners who want gardens filled with glorious plants, and experienced gardeners like myself who are taking their gardens into unknown territory. I predict that first you'll enjoy this book, then you'll *really* enjoy the new life it helps you create just outside your back door. Your front door, too. Go for it!

Susan Harris, co-founder of the team blog GardenRant
and founder of the Lawn Reform Coalition

preface

as a nature lover who also happens to enjoy gardening, I have been avidly studying, experimenting with, and having conversations about lawn alternatives ever since I bought my first house (and lawn). During the year in which I assembled the photos and wrote the text for this book, I came to appreciate anew the diverse personalities of gardens and their gardeners, and the stories that both contain.

A garden is a dynamic art form that depends on people for its ongoing life. The art does not exist merely within the garden but is also held and nurtured within the soul of the gardener; a real and powerful part of any garden is the relationship between it and the people who cherish it.

I have seen the heart go out of gardens whose gardener moved away. I have felt the amplified energy of gardens that are loved and cared for by a group of people. There are so many ways that a place can be enlivened by connections with people that I hesitate to say, as I once did, that land left to its own devices will be more full of life than land that is intensively cared for by people.

And that gives me hope that, in the future, our landscapes will be as varied and alive and artful and touching as the people who shape them. All that we need to do is rediscover the many wonderful things that can happen when you take a serious interest in your landscape's individual character and its good health. These revelations are what this book is really about.

acknowledgments

Many thanks to those who have contributed important ideas and inspiration to this book through their photos: Kelly Broich, Lucy Dinsmore, Jeff Epping, Billy Goodnick, Diane Hilscher, Lindsay Rebhan, Michael Schumacher, Lisa Weidema, and most especially to the poetic and philosophical Saxon Holt.

My deep appreciation goes to the many supportive and insightful people who have helped with thinking, organizing, and generating ideas and solutions for this book: Jason Doran, Fran Kiesling, Billy Goodnick, Karen Graham, Susan Harris, Diane Hilscher, Angela Hohler, Saxon Holt, Susan Morrison, Erik James Olsen, Nancy Schumacher, Carmen Simonet, Ginny Stibolt, Paula Westmoreland, and Peggy Willenberg. I am particularly indebted to dear friends Julie Kostroski and Kristin Matthews Long, and to my amazing, admirable sister Sherilyn, for pivotal conversations. Also my sincere thanks to the gardeners and designers whose stories fill these pages. All have provided crucial details and corrections; the text is much better for their gentle feedback and helpful suggestions.

Thanks to Susan Carpenter, native plant specialist at University of Wisconsin-Madison Arboretum; Don Cisler, head gardener/horticulturist at West of the Lake Gardens; Barbara DeGroot, public relations specialist, and Duane Otto, landscape gardener, at the Minnesota Landscape Arboretum; Janet Draper, horticulturist at Mary Livingston Ripley Garden; Jeff Epping, director of horticulture at Olbrich Botanical Gardens; Nancy Eshelman, proprietor of Morning Glory Inn in Pittsburgh; Randee Humphrey, director of education at Lewis Ginter Botanical Garden; Mary Meyer and Robert Mugaas, extension educators at the University of Minnesota; and other experts who answered my endless questions and waxed poetic about gardens, gardening, nature, and people's roles in different types of landscapes.

Kaitlen Brennan and Channing McKinley have my heartfelt gratitude for keeping me well and sane during the time that I wrote this book, and for several years leading up to it.

Thank you so much to my hard-working research assistants Julie Kostroski and Maggie Moffett. Thanks also to my models: Sarah, Phillip, Natalie, Levi, Doug, and Clara.

I am grateful to my editor Juree Sondker for making the project run smoothly, and to gem-cutter Franni Farrell for the work and love she heaped on this manuscript. Working with Timber Press has been a dream come true.

Thank you, Mom, forever and for everything.

Last but not least, I want to thank George, who has loved and believed in me for many years now, and who has made it possible for me to do work that I adore in the context of a balanced and fulfilling life. How lucky I am!

*A backyard can hold a lawn
…or a couple of patios, a
couple of woodlands, a prairie walk, and a pond.*

introduction

for the past century, we gardeners have loved our lawns. They have grown from an occasional play area (or status symbol) for the richest among us to a ubiquitous "affordable" groundcover. But the tide is turning. For a variety of reasons, from our changing environmental awareness to our changing lifestyles, some of us are shrinking our lawns. Others are leaving them behind altogether.

you don't need a lawn

In different areas of our diverse land, the local climate makes it hard to grow a healthy lawn. It may not be practical or worth the cost to give traditional turfgrass the care it needs to grow in those places, especially when we realize that drinkable water is becoming more scarce and water restrictions are on the rise. One easy first step to conserving potable water is to stop irrigating our lawns with it. Instead we can spread succulents, desert flowers, meadow and prairie gardens, and other dry-adapted landscapes across the drier midwestern, intermountain, and southwestern regions of this continent. We can hang a hammock in the shade of a vine-clad arbor and watch hummingbirds feasting on nectar and battling over all the new nesting sites we created by planting native shrubs.

Those of us who have the good fortune to live near a lake or stream are coming to understand that mown lawns can direct pollutant-laden runoff straight into the water, and are restoring our shorelines to naturalistic wetlands and woodlands. We hear the difference in the varied voices of waterbirds that repopulate those refurbished shorelines. They now have perches, cover, and food supplied by insects on land and water, plus fish that flourish in the clean water.

Through our successful efforts to help monarch butterflies by planting milkweed "waystations" all along their migration routes, and to bring bluebird populations back from the brink of extinction by building special houses for them, we have seen evidence that even one landowner on one small city lot can make an enormous difference to the survival of other species. Every one of us can take action in our own yard to help conserve global biodiversity, expand our urban forests, mitigate climate change, and at the same time make life richer and more fulfilling for our families and ourselves.

It used to be that only serious gardeners would take on the challenge of straying from the default home landscape of lawn and foundation plantings. Well, more of us are serious about gardening nowadays; a number of folks who might not lift a finger for an ornamental plant are determined to put in the effort of growing some of their own food. And luckily, even busy non-gardeners who don't have the time or desire to learn can find local resources and examples to help them exchange their lawns for satisfying alternative landscapes.

Lawn alternatives have always been around, but now with the tools and materials available—not to mention skilled experts for hire—there are more reasons than ever to bypass a lawn and choose something else. Whether you remove all your lawn or just a part of it, you can add new beauty, comfort, and ease to your life.

our changing definition of beauty

We've all heard that beauty is in the eye of the beholder, but an enjoyable landscape isn't simply a pretty picture with the right colors and a strong design. We do more than look at landscapes, after all. We walk through them. We sit in them. We appreciate them with all our senses.

Different landscapes appeal to different people. Some enjoy a view of mountains, while others like to see to the horizon. For some, color is everything. For others, dramatic shapes and textures are more important. Without even realizing it, we all respond to subtle cues in our surroundings: the pattern of dappled light coming through the trees, the distant sound of trickling water, the changing barometric pressure that precedes a thunderstorm. These messages from our senses cause us to have certain feelings about a place.

Familiarity is also part of what makes something (or someone) beautiful to us. So landscapes dominated by lawns may feel safe and welcoming if we have grown up with them, and other kinds of landscapes may be less appealing because they don't feel like home.

But as we come to know a place (or person) better, our opinion can change. A wooded landscape may feel oppressive at first if we are used to seeing the sky, but on spending more time among the trees, we may come to appreciate them as havens from the sun and wind, sources of scents that permeate the garden, or nesting places for the songbirds that serenade us each morning. We can grow to love a mossy glade that we can sink our bare feet into, or the soothing murmur of the ocean, or the way the wind ruffles meadow grass, just as we come to adore a friend who always surprises us into a laugh, a neighbor who brings a fresh-baked pie, or a child who reawakens our curiosity about the world.

A lush and colorful dry-adapted hillside presents an attractive alternative to thirsty lawns and gravel-dominated xeriscapes.

In the Midwest, homeowners are embracing a new aesthetic with prairie gardens like this one, which replaced an unused suburban front lawn and features regionally adapted plants that thrive without supplemental water.

Our tastes are swayed by the people who surround us. Through the history of garden-making, different styles and elements have been preferred by certain cultures. A water feature was expected in an Arabian courtyard garden. Asian-style gardens, traditional and modern, embrace rocks and shun exuberant floral displays. And in North America, until quite recently, lush green lawns have been widely admired.

The pressure to conform to the widespread preference for lawns still exists; in some places, it is nothing less than unpatriotic to think of removing your front lawn and putting in a wild mix of vegetables and flowers. However, in more and more city blocks, neighborhoods, metropolitan areas, watersheds, and even entire regions, new and diverse aesthetics are evolving.

returning life to our landscapes

In a way, our lawns reflect our modern lives. Some people prefer cyberspace and temperature-controlled buildings to the mysterious, often messy outdoors. Fear of strangers and aversion to annoyances like biting bugs and humidity—coupled with an unlimited supply of TV shows, crafts, organized events, and other attractive ways to spend an evening—are making us less interested in going out to watch the stars or the sunset. If you live in an urban area, chances are you cannot see them anyway.

The outdoors is often just space that we move through on our way from appointment to appointment. We may not spend much time there. Many of us don't have landscapes that are interesting enough to pull us away from electronic devices and screens and the rest of our human-generated indoor world. Lawns certainly aren't interesting enough to do that.

Here's why: *life* is what interests us.

Human beings have a natural affinity for other forms of life. Another living creature draws our attention in any type of setting, and most of us want to see birds, butterflies, and other animals as well as plants in our landscapes. Life—in all its variability, changeability, and potential to surprise and delight—is beautiful. And life is what our lawns are missing.

Biologically speaking, our lawns are nearly dead. Only a handful of plant and animal species (such as Kentucky bluegrass, grubs, and robins here in Minnesota) are able to survive the chemical applications and cutting regimens we commonly practice when we aim for perfect turf. Lawns won't ever fade away completely; they will always be the preferred flooring for some types of outdoor play, and they will continue to be grown in the few regions where they thrive with little care. But we are collectively realizing that perfect lawns are unnecessary for most of us, and that the price we pay for them in clean water and urban serenity is far too high.

We have converted thousands upon thousands of acres of land from wild areas into turf, so much land that lawn is now recognized as the "largest irrigated crop" in the United States. Compacted urban and suburban lawns shed stormwater, contributing to runoff that is causing swollen streams to erode their banks, lakes and wetlands to flood nearby areas, and precious topsoil to be swept downriver and lost to our oceans. The chemical fertilizers and pesticides we use on our lawns have polluted our surface water and contaminated our groundwater. Meanwhile, motorized mowers and blowers create noise and air pollution in our neighborhoods.

Our lawns also cost too much in terms of our own schedules and pocketbooks. With lives that are busier than ever before, painstakingly grooming turf (or paying someone to do it) has become a luxury and pastime shared by fewer and fewer homeowners. As we tighten our belts in the shrinking modern economy, we are putting our money toward our top priorities and trimming unnecessary expenses. Just think, you won't need to keep trimming that lawn if you trim it out of your budget!

Where we need open spaces to play, periodically

mown fields would do just as well in most cases, at much lower cost. When you are running after a ball, you don't stop to count the dandelions. And we also need places for doing things besides playing ball. Like watching the dragonflies, or picking a fresh organic lunch, or reading this book outside in a lawn chair with a tall cool drink.

We are the ones who bring life to our lawns—with a game, or a picnic, or a party with a tent and tables and chairs and food and music…Lawns are merely outdoor carpets on which we carry out the business of living our lives.

In contrast, a lawnless or less-lawn landscape can fascinate us with its beauty, complexity, and variability. It can cool us in the summer and hoard warmth in the winter. It can open our senses to new aromas and flavors, sounds and textures. It can be a window into the daily lives of an astonishing variety of other creatures. It can spur us to wonder and to explore. It can revive our bodies and recharge our minds. Far beyond just providing an open-air stage for our lives, a robust and vibrant landscape can enrich them immeasurably.

the future of the north american lawn

Ours is a continent with remarkable variety of climates, topographies, and ecologies. When we spend time outdoors, we don't all wear the same clothes or pursue the same activities. How could we expect the same landscape to fit everybody's needs?

Just as we have learned to accept and appreciate many different cultures in our new world melting pot, we are learning to welcome (or at least tolerate) diversity in our yards and public landscapes. Those of us who still love lawns are learning to accept that some of the neighbors may not love them too. Those of us who feel all lawns should be eliminated are learning to accept that for some, a lawn is central to their desired lifestyle. We are in the

process of redefining lawns as just one of many possible landscape elements, to be used when the situation dictates, rather than as the only socially acceptable choice for certain places. These changes in our landscaping styles are coming hand-in-hand with a new appreciation for our regional plants and animals, and for the characteristic landscapes of the areas in which we live.

When we realize that lawns aren't a required part of a landscape, we are free to create (or leave untouched) places that inspire us, that make it easier and more pleasant to spend time outdoors. We can invite birds and other wildlife back into our yards. We can breathe fresh air and grow fresh food to share with our families and friends. We can fix or prevent drainage issues caused by stormwater running across our properties. We can restore nearby water bodies to pristine health and productivity. We can admire the drama of the ever-changing seasons.

We can bring the natural world back into our yards, our neighborhoods, and our daily lives.

rethinking your yard

Some of our prime growing sites, relatively free of trees and warmed by surrounding pavement, are located in our front yards. Often these valuable spaces go unused. Fitted with a pristine green carpet, they remain as empty as a formal dining room that gathers dust while the family crowds around a too-small kitchen table. Meanwhile, the real living happens in backyards that are crowded with play areas, seating areas, flowerbeds, and vegetable patches, all in less-than-ideal sizes and locations.

But one by one, these unused front lawns are giving way to gardens. If you have a small yard, why not make it *all* livable? Plenty of creative ideas can turn unloved lawn into a paradise. Use shrubs or a fence and a vine-covered arbor to transform your skinny side yard into a secret garden. Grow islands of raspberries in your lawn to give you easy access and keep them from spreading. Plant

a woodland garden around your patio for shelter and privacy, shade and birdsong, and all-season interest. And in your sunniest spot—wherever it happens to be—grow edibles for fresh snacks, healthy meals, and sharing.

On larger properties, lawns have been stretched to cover acres of land that once held woodlands, prairies and meadows, wetlands, deserts, and other natural areas. Hours of our valuable time are spent mowing these places that no person uses. This unnecessary labor has the unfortunate effect of disrupting valuable environmental services and erasing wildlife habitat.

But one by one, our lifeless landscapes are being re-vived. If you have a large property, why not share it with other species? Give yourself and your mower a rest, and invite plants and animals back to outlying areas. Once the natural splendor of these places is restored, you might find them more inviting too. You might take up hiking, or bird watching, or fishing, or nature photography. You might recapture your sense of wonder…or you might simply feel relieved, free from the burden of intensively managing every square foot of your property.

In cities and suburbs from coast to coast, people are creating a dazzling array of gardens with smaller lawns or no lawns at all. They are using innovative elements and combinations to make places like no other. They are reinterpreting or relying on time-honored styles. They are restoring landscapes to naturalistic communities. They are preserving gardens that were made by previous generations and have never included lawns. These varied gardens and their gardeners are a boundless source of inspiration.

Each of the gardens in this book was chosen to high-light specific ideas and strategies. You can adapt and use what you learn from them even if their style or region is different from yours. Probably you will not find a garden that you could or would want to copy exactly, because the garden that fits your needs, your climate, and your taste will be unique.

As your vision takes shape in your mind, and as you begin bringing it to life in your landscape, remember that design is an ongoing process. Even the best designer will tell you that he or she simply installs the garden, but those who live with it will come to know it best and will refine it over time. Successful gardens—those that are used and appreciated—are continually evolving to fit our changing needs and lifestyle, our growing wisdom, and the vagaries of nature.

So don't worry about getting it just right. Making a garden is not like laying tile or hanging wallpaper. The more you know about your garden's peculiar needs and gifts, the better choices you will make about what to do in your landscape, or whether to do anything at all.

And here's a secret: no matter how hard you work and how much money you spend, your garden will never be perfect. But you will love it anyway. You will love it like you never loved a lawn.

top: Rather than looking out onto a flat stretch of lawn or pavement, you can vertically layer plants to bring nature up to your windows and doors. A surprising number of plants will fit in a small space.

bottom: Even a modest urban herb plot adds dispropor-tionate richness to daily life.

part one
design inspiration:
the many possibilities

From the Pacific Northwest to the Florida Keys, people are creating lawnless gardens to suit a broad range of sites, tastes, and lifestyles. This first section of the book shares some of these inspiring gardens, the stories behind them, and words of wisdom from the gardeners themselves. Each chapter showcases a different possibility for lawnless design, from living carpets to (for those who don't want to give them up) the next generation of smarter lawns. In every chapter you can visit gardens vicariously…more than 50 examples of beautiful, sustainable, lawnless gardens!

This two-year-old suburban front garden already provides drifts of colorful blooms, grasses that catch the light, and evergreens for four-season interest.

living carpets

W hat if you could replace all or part of your lawn with a low, living carpet of plants that would never need mowing, water, or fertilizer? Plants that would green up earlier than your lawn every spring, maybe even stay green all winter. Plants that could stay dense and healthy in the shade, or take summer's heat and drought without going dormant or dying off altogether. What if these plants also flowered once a year or had aromatic foliage? What if they attracted butterflies?

*A sea of deadnettle (*Lamium maculatum*) flows around the occasional hosta, making a peaceful living carpet that blooms, supports wildlife, and never needs mowing.*

No matter where your garden is located, no matter what your site conditions, there are plants that will do these things for you. Maybe you won't find one plant that will do them all, but then again, maybe you will. Try sweet woodruff (*Galium odoratum*) in the damp, shady area on the east side of your house; creeping yarrow (*Achillea ageratifolia*) or a mix of low sedums in a hot, dry spot surrounded by pavement; lilyturf (*Liriope*) under your big southern magnolia; strawberries (*Fragaria*) and winecups (*Callirhoe*) running down your slope; dwarf crested iris (*Iris cristata*) on a boggy bank…and so many more.

With a little research and a one-time conversion, you could be living a different life outdoors. You could stop cutting down grass and then encouraging it to grow and then cutting it down again. Instead, you could spend your time stretched out on a blanket listening to crickets chirp while the leaves of your locust tree flutter above you. The changing of the seasons would no longer bring to mind a chemical concoction that must

top left: Each September, under the fruiting branches of an ornamental crabapple (Malus sargentii), autumn crocus (Colchicum 'Lilac Wonder') emerges from a carpet of purpleleaf winter-creeper (Euonymus fortunei 'Coloratus') at Olbrich Botanical Gardens, Madison, Wisconsin.

top right: Susan Harris replaced her oval-shaped front lawn with a mix of low-growing groundcov-ers, including creeping jenny (Lysimachia num-mularia) and sweet alyssum (Lobularia maritima).

bottom left: Stepping stones lead from the house to the back woods, through a once-living carpet of white clover (Trifolium repens) and creeping sedum (S. sarmentosum).

bottom right: A diverse, four-season border of shrubs, trees, and perennials keeps this garden interesting and beautiful while the gardener experiments with living carpets.

be added to your lawn, or a note to change the oil in your mower; you could anticipate more pleasant sea-sonal events like the spicy scent of mint underfoot or the sunset-colored haze that appears above purple love grass (*Eragrostis spectabilis*) from midsummer to frost.

Every square foot of your property would no longer be under your thumb. The plants would be free to grow naturally to their mature sizes, undergoing seasonal changes and perhaps even reproducing, and you would be free to enjoy them.

a lawn alternative testing ground

Susan Harris has been gardening on her property just outside Washington, D.C., since 1985, and for most of that time, she maintained lawns in both the front and back yards. But as happens in so many gardens, her borders expanded each year and her lawns shrank. As she became more interested in lawn alternatives, particu-larly through her work spearheading the Lawn Reform Coalition, Susan decided to replace her front lawn with a beautiful and low-care living carpet.

She used a flat-edged spade to dig out the grass ("It made great compost," she says) and planted a mix of low, ornamental groundcovers. Thus began her ongoing struggle to create a living carpet that would have enough color and interest for a front yard without demanding too much care. Plants have come and gone; her oval is currently filled with groundcover sedums in a variety of colors and forms. Unlike many of the plants that failed her—including creeping thyme—the sedums can with-stand the baking heat and weeks of drought typical of her zone 7 location. This is one reason they are preferred roof garden plants.

As sedums have sparser foliage than some other living carpets, Susan's main maintenance challenge in the future might be keeping the weeds out of her sedum lawn. Mulching with wood chips would cover bare ground and deter weeds, but it would also keep the ground too moist for these dry-adapted plants. Though hand-weeding works for now, Susan is thinking ahead, realizing that, at a certain point, it will become more difficult to bend and pull the weeds. She is considering a handheld fire wand; because the sedums are succulents, the high proportion of water in their leaves makes them fire-tolerant.

Susan is also trialing alternative lawns in her sloping backyard, which is reached by a short flight of steps. Weary of carting her mower up and down the steps, she

finally tore out the turf grass and replaced it with a mix of white clover (*Trifolium repens*) and a non-native creeping sedum (*S. sarmentosum*) that has naturalized in sunny areas around her neighborhood. This new lawn seemed ideal for the first few months. It required no mowing, bloomed in bright yellow and white, and was flat and tough enough to walk on. But over the course of the summer, the clover outcompeted the sedum, then it died during a not-uncommon late summer drought, leaving her new "lawn" mostly bare.

Susan responded in the classic way that experienced gardeners do: she declared the clover a failure, pulled what remained of it, and added more starts of the sedum. It is after all a lovely chartreuse color, her favorite.

In the garden, things don't always work out the way you hope. Susan will continue to patiently fine-tune her two living carpets until she finds plants that can stay low, take light foot traffic, and withstand her climate. And while she's experimenting, she's still able to enjoy her large, healthy mixed borders; these offer satisfying color and interest through the seasons with only minimal care.

You may be one of the millions of gardeners or homeowners like Susan, someone who wants to replace their lawn but isn't sure what plants to replace it with, or how to maintain them. If so, you are the reason this book exists. Because every site is different, you too will need to do some experimenting in your own garden, but you can save time, money, and frustration by learning from the experiences of the gardeners in the following pages.

diversity with mini-monocultures

We often hear environmentalists and gardeners decrying the perfect chemically maintained lawn because it is a stand of a single plant species, a monoculture. While diversity does make a healthier and more environmentally sound landscape, you don't have to mix plants together to increase your yard's diversity. Another approach is to plant in patches or drifts, each of them a mini-monoculture. This can make your maintenance easier and give your yard a more serene look.

Minnesota gardener Marte Hult has converted much of her suburban lawn to mini-monocultures. She has gradually shrunk her lawn by adding islands around each of her large trees. For each island, she used a different carpet of a single groundcover. She started ten years ago with her two apple trees, replacing the lawn under them "because it was hard to mow under there and the grass didn't grow well anyway."

Marte's house sits on a hill, with a level front yard and a backyard that slopes down away from the house. Her largest and most glamorous mini-monoculture is the expanse of bugleweed (*Ajuga reptans*) that cascades down the steepest part of the back slope. This was an area that she and her husband, Mike, were not fond of mowing, and now it has become a much-anticipated seasonal feature of their garden. The bugleweed bursts into flower in early spring, covering itself in pink and purple blooms just when color is most needed in a northern garden. Even after the flowers have passed, it makes an attractive groundcover, with its thick green and purple foliage flowing alongside the staircase and between the patio stones.

Marte's bugleweed was originally planted around a willow tree that has since died of old age. Luckily, this groundcover withstood the change from heavy shade to full sun, though such a drastic shift in site conditions would set back less adaptable plants. To fill in after the tree stump was removed, Marte dug out sections from thick patches of bugleweed and planted them in bare spots. Within a year, it was hard to tell a tree had been there.

Another of her tree islands is carpeted with pachysandra (*P. terminalis*), and across the walk from it, a variegated form of yellow archangel (*Lamiastrum galeobdolon*) surrounds another tree. Taller than the bugleweed, it blooms around the same time, but with yellow flowers. Over the years Marte has added a carpet of creeping thyme, a path

This sedum-clover mix, dense, low, walkable, and colorful, made an ideal alternative lawn that never needed mowing—until the clover died in a drought.

Even when it isn't flowering, bugleweed makes an ornamental, low-care lawn alternative. It also fills gaps and deters weeds between flagstones next to the back patio.

A good way to start shrinking the lawn is to add islands around your trees. Here, each island is a mini-monoculture, so weeding and other maintenance are minimized, but each is also a different species, bringing diversity to the garden.

of stepping stones padded with low woolly thyme, and a large bed of bearded iris—her favorites—growing up through various companion plants.

Once established, minimal maintenance is required for these hardy groundcovers. Marte deadheads the bugleweed because it occupies such a central location in her garden, but if she didn't, the plant's brown seedheads would crumble and be engulfed by the foliage. Any weed that pokes through the heavy cover of yellow archangel or pachysandra is quickly dispatched. Groundcovers that wander into the paths are dug out.

These mini-monocultures allow views across the entire garden, and they feel as neat and tidy as miniature lawns, only with more colorful foliage and seasonal flowers to liven them up. They are not walkable like lawns, but Marte has built paths through them. She converts a new section of her lawn to garden space every year by solarizing it with a piece of black plastic. She leaves the plastic down for a whole year. While she concentrates on other garden projects, it transforms her lawn into soil. When she is ready to plant the new garden space, she moves the black plastic to cover another area, making another new garden space for next year.

Marte's mini-monocultures relieve her of a large portion of her lawn, leaving her with more time for work and hobbies, and for relaxing in her gazebo with a coffee or a cocktail at hand. She says, "What I like best about my garden is how I feel when I am in it. My favorite garden saying is 'I live in the garden—I only sleep in the house.'" Her approach is a simple way to start if you're not a gardener. You won't need to learn about a lot of different plants, and you can keep maintenance low, provided you choose vigorous plants that can be kept in check with one or two clippings or weed patrols a year.

wall to wall

Marte's various living "throw rugs" did the trick for her, but if you want wall-to-wall coverage, there are certain spots where it's easy to make a better choice than a lawn. Take slopes, for instance, where a lawn invites traffic that may be unwanted, mowing may be risky, and short grass doesn't prevent runoff from spilling onto whatever lies downhill.

Yet a slope offers many prime gardening opportunities and can be a prominent feature in your garden. It can bring little plants closer to eye level, allowing you to appreciate them without stooping. For the gardener who craves diversity, a slope offers an array of microclimates you can't find in a flat, uniform stretch of ground. The top of a slope is drier and well-drained, the north side is

In a small urban front yard, a slope of succulents including yellow-flowering bush sedum (S. dendroideum subsp. praealtum), blue finger (Senecio mandraliscae), and velvet rose (Aeonium 'Mint Saucer') offers a bold and beautiful view from the sidewalk.

protected from hot sun, the base is cooler and moister. This diversity of microclimates increases the variety of plants you can grow.

You may have a small or medium-sized garden with a pleasing structure and year-round appeal, and you just need a groundcover for that square that you've hedged, or to fill that skinny fragment of land between the garage and the sidewalk. You don't care if it looks like a lawn as long as it is dense enough to deter weeds and stays green for as much of the year as possible. Plenty of plants meet these criteria, but you may be tempted to overlook them because they are commonly used. Visit old-fashioned formal gardens and Asian-style gardens to see how well these old standbys contribute their steady green support to a strong design. You will see beds of ivy (*Hedera*), pachysandra (*P. terminalis*), sweet woodruff (*Galium odoratum*), wild gingers (*Asarum canadense, A. europaeum*), creeping juniper (*Juniperus horizontalis*), sweet box (*Sarcococca hookeriana* var. *humilis*), periwinkle (*Vinca minor*), and other humble, hard-working plants that modern gardeners may be tempted to snub. In these gardens, their value is obvious: by not drawing attention to themselves, they leave your eyes and mind free to drift over a peaceful green expanse. How refreshing.

It may be that you just want a green, wall-to-wall, living carpet to do what a lawn would do: flow around your trees, alongside the driveway, and basically across any ground not already covered by plants or hard surfaces. You won't need to mow if you choose a dense, low-growing groundcover, or perhaps a mix of them. You can forego the watering as well, by selecting from the large pool of groundcovers that are more drought-tolerant than commonly used turfgrasses. Unlike the turfgrasses, many groundcovers will keep their color through the growing season without going brown and dormant in dry spells.

Some fine-leaved groundcovers look like lawns, especially from a distance, except once a year when they metamorphose into showy flowering carpets. Many of these lawn look-alikes can bounce back if occasionally walked across, though they may not stand up to regular foot traffic. They include creeping phlox (*P. subulata*), creeping thyme (*Thymus serpyllum*), mondo grass (*Ophiopogon japonicus*) and its selection 'Nanus' (dwarf mondo), lilyturf (*Liriope spicata, L. muscari,* and others), and low sedums. For a more durable path that will add visual interest and keep your feet drier too, place stepping stones in your groundcover. Direct them to your lawn chair, or to a picnic table that is big enough for the whole family (and that you will never need to move in order to mow the lawn).

If you find it necessary to keep a large area free of trees, or retain a clear view across an area, some groundcovers are up to the task of substituting for a large expanse of lawn. For the work of periodically weeding out tree seedlings or unwanted ground-layer plants (how often will depend on your groundcover's vigor and nearby weed sources), you could be rewarded with less or no mowing, less or no watering, and the potential to improve soil health, wildlife habitat, and four-season interest.

In a large area that is not used as a ball field, where the plants don't need to withstand intensive traffic, your choice of plants will be broad. And a groundcover that might not hold up under soccer games could still be walked on (or played on or picnicked on) and then allowed to recover.

Don't overlook low shrubs as easy and effective groundcovers. A shrubby groundcover gives a subtle (or obvious, depending on the shrub) signal to stay off an area. This can be useful where you want to restrict pedestrian traffic, such as in planting beds alongside walkways or in places where people may be tempted to shortcut across the garden. You might use a barrier of low shrubs to guard delicate plants against foot traffic, while keeping them visible from the path.

Asiatic jasmine (Trachelospermum asiaticum) makes a low, easy-care lawn substitute in a lawnless public park.

Bigroot geranium (G. macrorrhizum 'Ingwersen's Variety') has effectively held its ground for a quarter century with minimal care under oak and maple trees at the Minnesota Landscape Arboretum.

top: After the flowers are gone and the tree leaves have fallen, the geranium's multi-hued autumn foliage contributes color to the landscape for weeks.

bottom: Bearberry (including Arctostaphylos uva-ursi *'Radiant', shown here) is a model four-season groundcover for well-drained, sunny spots. With tiny, leathery evergreen leaves, pink flowers in spring, and red berries for the birds in summer, what's not to love? Oh, and bearberry needs no mowing, no fertilizer, and little or no water from you.*

Low evergreen shrubs can provide year-round protection against soil erosion and cover for small creatures. If you do not appreciate the rugged appearance of the commonly used carpet junipers, there are plenty of other very different-looking low evergreens with a variety of foliage colors and textures. Some are dense and dark, like yew (*Taxus*) and boxwood (*Buxus*), while others are more open-textured, like the lacy panels of Siberian cypress (*Microbiota decussata*). Some needled plants feel soft; try running your fingers along the tufted branches of a dwarf hemlock (*Tsuga canadensis* 'Gentsch White' or similar).

Low deciduous shrubs offer a chance for a changing look through the seasons. The deciduous cranberry cotoneaster (*C. apiculatus*) has arching branches and red berries, and its foliage turns a deep maroon in fall. The winter fruit of coralberry (*Symphoricarpos orbiculatus*) gives a welcome spot of color, and snowberry (*S. albus*) provides food for ground birds like turkeys and pheasants. Especially useful on slopes and in larger areas, quick-spreading dwarf fragrant sumac (*Rhus aromatica* 'Gro-Low') makes a spectacular fall display. Lowbush blueberry (*Vaccinium angustifolium*) grows well in acidic soil and has dainty spring flowers, edible fruits, and bronze-red fall color.

Save your intensively maintained lawn for smaller areas, where you'll be sure to see your efforts rewarded as it is used and loved. For areas that are used less frequently or less intensively, choose a wall-to-wall carpet that performs services that aren't in a lawn's repertoire, like offering seasonal (maybe even year-round) shows, providing nectar for pollinators or berries for birds, and giving you a break from mowing and watering.

spice it up

One of the fun things about gardening is playing with color. Some low groundcovers that make fine alternatives to lawn have a showy, non-green foliage color all through the year. This presents an opportunity to design a bolder and more dramatic garden, if you dare. Try red and gold sedums, white artemisias (for instance, *A. stelleriana* 'Silver Brocade'), dark-leaved bugleweed or black mondo grass (*Ophiopogon planiscapus* 'Nigrescens'), variegated Asiatic jasmine (*Trachelospermum asiaticum* 'Variegatum'), or Japanese painted fern (*Athyrium niponicum* var. *pictum*). Pick a color that contrasts nicely with or sets off the colors in your garden, including buildings and other structures.

Some groundcovers add color by flowering during part of the year or changing their foliage colors in the fall. This adds complexity to your design, and it gives you a chance to plan color combinations for different seasons. For instance, a carpet of white-blooming false spirea (*Astilbe ×arendsii*) under white-trunked paper birches has extra punch when the false spirea is blooming, and also in autumn when the leaves of both plants turn yellow.

No matter which groundcovers you choose, you may be able to find plants that will grow up through your living carpet and add a flare of color during one season or another. Bulbs can give a ho-hum green groundcover an extra season of showiness, without adding to the workload. Make sure they are tall enough to rise above your ground-layer plants. Most bulbs are adapted to push their leaves and stems up through a blanket of dry leaves or grasses, so they can push through a groundcover too. Their flowers can be chosen to extend your season of bloom, or to bloom along with the groundcover and amplify your color display.

You can also plant perennials through your living carpet. A few accents will draw attention and can be strategically placed to lead the eyes toward a focal point,

Self-sowing lupines (Lupinus Russell hybrids), descended from one seed packet sown several years ago, add spice to this low sedum lawn. The gardener says, "When the seedpod gets ripe, it twists as it bursts open, scattering the seeds a good distance. Sounds like popcorn on a warm afternoon!"

or to divert them from an unappealing view. An entire overstory of perennials above your living carpet can add wildlife habitat as well as a variety of textures and colors through the seasons.

Self-sowing plants—whether annual, biennial, or perennial—offer plenty of scope for fun and inexpensive garden experiments. Sow their seeds over the top of your groundcover, or plant some seedlings in it, and watch new plants pop up in unexpected places in future years. You may need to help them spread by scattering their seeds each year, or to curtail their spread by clipping off their flowers before they set seed, or by pulling some seedlings. Self-sowers that you choose to mingle with your groundcover must be able to germinate in its shade. Go ahead, play a little, and see if you can find a good mix for your garden.

shade gardens

Add interest and habitat with vertical layers. Susan Harris' woodland garden includes a ground layer of variegated solomon's seal (Polygonatum odoratum var. thunbergii 'Variegatum'), Japanese painted fern (Athyrium niponicum var. pictum), and white-blooming Virginia sweetspire (Itea virginica) under taller shrubs and trees.

a woodland can be a deeply affecting place. Shade and stillness seem to go hand in hand; they promote an opening of our senses to catch the subtle cues of lower levels of light and movement. Consciously or not, we are more present, more aware of our surroundings, and therefore more receptive to them. The woodland gardener can play to this enhanced awareness and make a memorable garden that has real power to soothe.

Woodland gardens offer us comfort. We appreciate shade during the sunniest seasons and shelter from wind and light rain; these amenities may encourage us to spend more time out in the garden. Layers of greenery are especially welcome in an urban setting, where they filter and purify the air and obscure hard walls and floors.

You can augment the peaceful mood of your shady haven by silencing your own urban noise. Trees appreciate undisturbed root zones teeming with microbial life, and throughout their long lives they develop partnerships with many other organisms, from underground mycorrhizal fungi to migrating birds. These connections can be severed by overzealous gardening. Woodland gardeners can contribute to their trees' health by refraining from mowing, blowing, raking, and much other tidying.

The comforts of the woodland garden can be felt and brought indoors as well. Plant trees to shade your roof and the heat-catching pavement of driveways and patios; trees can cool the air under their canopies by five to 25 degrees Fahrenheit, and this can translate into not only comfort but significant savings on your air conditioning costs. To make

Fringed bergenia (B. ciliata) and Tiny Tim euphorbia (E. martinii 'Waleutiny') add textural diversity to a shady site at the Ripley Garden, Smithsonian Institution, Washington, D.C.

the biggest difference, target any window that lets in the intense afternoon rays of the summer sun. Shading the outside of the building is even more effective than using curtains or blinds inside the house, plus it means you can fall asleep with the fresh scent of pine trees drifting in through your open bedroom window.

Shady sites give a creative gardener so many elements to play with. You can venture into architecture, using tree islands, groves, and clearings to shape interesting and inviting spaces. You can catch, block, and filter light, creating shifts that lend distinct moods to your garden spaces. In any shade garden, foliage will be a major contributor of visual interest, with a variety of plant forms available and any number of vertical layers in which to plant them. A creative gardener can find ways to add color even in shade if desired, but don't overlook the pleasures gained from varied textures and hues of foliage, wood, and rock.

for the birds

Inspired by her work with The Nature Conservancy, which protects and preserves our world's priceless natural places, Michelle Kalantari decided to bring more life—both plants and animals—into her urban yard. She lives in a neighborhood populated with mature native silver maples (*Acer saccharinum*), and several grow on her 50- by 125-foot property, so it was natural to pattern her garden after a woodland.

Being a bird lover, Michelle wanted to attract a wider array of songbirds to her yard. Her large trees were limbed up, their lower branches removed to let in more light, giving her room to add understory plants and grow some showier flowers that tolerate part shade. A key component of her garden is an assortment of shrubs, which provide nesting places and food—in the form of insects, seeds, and berries—for the birds. Another important element is the lowest layer of plants, which protects the soil from erosion, harbors spiders and other beneficial bugs that prey on pest insects, and makes it safer and more comfortable for small creatures to move easily through the garden.

Michelle's garden was designed by Paula Westmoreland, founder of the landscape design firm Ecological Gardens in Minneapolis. Paula specializes in creating landscapes that function like natural communities; she pays particular attention to generating healthy soil life, including a diverse mix of compatible plants, and building connections between the plants, animals, fungi, microbes, rocks, and other elements in a landscape.

Michelle's budget was limited, so she hired Paula to design the garden and to return and do the initial planting once the site was prepared. She started with the backyard, digging up all the existing sod, which was used to build several berms in the front yard. Her back garden has three main "rooms," each with a slightly different character. They all blend together in a space that feels much larger than it did when it was a lawn.

View of an urban backyard in 2007: the lawn is gone and the understory of a woodland garden has just been planted.

The furthest corner of Michelle's back garden features a stone bench surrounded by drifts of ostrich fern (*Matteuccia struthiopteris*) and lily-of-the-valley (*Convallaria majalis*). The back and sides of the bench are shielded by fences, native hazelnut shrubs (*Corylus americana*), and a tall trellis planted with a purple-flowering clematis. The fences are painted white, which lightens the area. The shrubs, still young, will grow up and provide more visual privacy and four-season structure for the garden, as well as additional nest sites for songbirds. This bench will eventually become a sheltered seat that offers a view across the entire garden.

The sunniest area of the backyard is also the liveliest and most colorful, hopping with entertaining birds and insects, and easily viewed from inside the house. Spreading out from several bird feeders are an assortment of showy flowers and grasses, including lavender-flowered anise hyssop (*Agastache foeniculum*), pale yellow coreopsis

*Sun-loving flowers and grasses offer nectar and food, attracting a parade of birds, butterflies, and hummingbirds. In the foreground are bright crimson bee balm (*Monarda didyma), *red cardinal flower (*Lobelia cardinalis), *and yellow-blooming yarrow (*Achillea millefolium).

(*C. verticillata* 'Moonbeam'), red flame grass (*Miscanthus sinensis* 'Purpurascens'), tufted hairgrass (*Deschampsia cespitosa*), and little bluestem (*Schizachyrium scoparium*). These attract delicious insects, which the birds can eat all year and feed to their young. Both the grasses and the flowers also develop seedheads, providing additional bird food during late summer, fall, and winter.

The third area is thickly carpeted with native wild strawberries (*Fragaria virginiana*) running among clusters of solomon's seal (*Polygonatum biflorum*) and other woodland wildflowers. It contains a large silver maple tree and a standing dead tree, or snag, which attracts wood-digesting insects and the woodpeckers that relish them. Michelle has trained a native American bittersweet vine (*Celastrus scandens*) up the snag, and the vine forms

Three years after planting, shrubs and ferns have filled in, and wild strawberries (Fragaria virginiana) clothe the ground (and produce edible fruit) under a vine-clad snag.

Given ample water and fertile soil, showy flowers including queen-of-the-prairie (Filipendula rubra), native wild bergamot (Monarda fistulosa), and turk's cap lily (Lilium superbum) thrive in the high shade cast by a limbed-up silver maple in the front yard.

While the morning sun's rays paint bright patches on neighboring lawns, in this lawnless front garden they illuminate golden foliage of spiderwort (Tradescantia 'Blue and Gold'), frosty blooms of foamflower (Tiarella cordifolia 'Pink Skyrocket'), and the mottled face of a large boulder.

a sheltered corridor for birds and other small animals to move up and down the trunk.

A few years after the backyard garden was planted, Michelle again enlisted Paula's help as she converted her entire front lawn into a wildlife-friendly shade garden. She put extra effort into making the garden visually appealing so that it would be easily accepted despite its dramatic departure from the neighborhood "norm." As in the backyard, limbing up the tall trees brought light into this garden and made room to add tall understory plants. The showiest tall flowers are sited to fill the view from inside the house with their colorful blooms and fluttering pollinators.

Though the garden contains mostly native plants because they support local wildlife, Michelle insisted that the design should have plenty of lilacs, lilies, zinnias, and other familiar, well-loved plants that her neighbors might enjoy. Paula compiled a community of plants that provide flowers and colorful foliage throughout the growing season, showy leaves and seedheads in late summer and fall, and berries through the year including winter. Now in its third year, the garden has filled out and gives a richly textured and dynamic visual display year-round.

Several large log pieces and a boulder are included in the garden. These non-living elements offer shelter for small creatures and food for insects, fungi, and birds. They also add textural interest and four-season structure to the garden in a natural-looking way. A path of log rounds blends in well as it leads explorers along the inner edge of the main berm. Visiting neighborhood children are especially drawn to this path, says Michelle.

As in the backyard, the plants were chosen to increase the diversity and abundance of insect life. This began as a feature to attract birds and encourage them to nest and raise young in the garden, but it has led Michelle to develop an interest in identifying and learning about her fascinating array of insect visitors. She has also honed her skill at photographing her garden and its inhabitants, and she presents slideshows to groups of gardeners, sharing her success story and introducing them to the many insects and plants that enliven her yard.

Having removed all the lawn from her property, Michelle is relieved not to have to mow during summer's heat and humidity, nor to rake up the copious maple leaves. She does rake up the maple whirlybirds in the spring after they fall from the trees, which means fewer maple seedlings to pull later in the year. She also "edits" the garden by digging up unwanted extra plants and giving them to friends and fellow gardeners.

After transforming her lawn into a naturalistic woodland garden, Michelle's workload diminished and her satisfaction soared. She says, "I feel like I'm surrounded by life now."

natural light show

Shady places bring opportunities to play with light. There is an ethereal quality to the rays that break through the upper canopy; they move across a shaded space as the day progresses, and every hour some new element catches the sun while the rest of the garden remains in shadow.

Jay Sifford has created a naturalistic woodland and water garden in Charlotte, North Carolina, in which dramatic shifts of sunlight take center stage. His emphasis on the movement of the light makes it a tangible presence in his garden.

When Jay moved in six years ago, the slope beside his house was "rotting railroad ties and mud." At first he tried to work with it, but then he decided to take advantage of the mature trees and steep grade to make a more natural landscape. "I am totally captivated by both the awesome splendor and the subtle nuances that nature throws our way," he says.

One element that Jay uses to bring in light is water. He hired Pete Johnson of Cascading Landscapes, who created three ponds connected by a natural-looking stream. The

ponds are built from sturdy retaining wall blocks with a facing of natural stone. By happy chance, many of the garden's ferns—a host of wood ferns (*Dryopteris*), including autumn fern (*D. erythrosora*), and a few Japanese painted ferns (*Athyrium niponicum* var. *pictum*)—arrived as spores on those stones. In addition to the reflective surface of the ponds, the stream has three separate waterfalls, each oriented in a different direction. These waterfalls catch light that enters the garden from different angles.

Jay's second method for catching light involves several panels he designed and erected behind his pondside seating area. The panels are made from wooden frames covered in backerboard, sealed with a cement sealant. They screen the view of the neighbor's tall house in a friendly

left: A woodland garden with artistic flair has transformed the slope between two houses.

right: Zigzagging waterfalls and textured panels behind a red bench catch and display shafts of sunlight.

left: You don't need flowers! Variegated hostas and annual coleus (Solenostemon) bathe this shade garden in light and color.

right: A murmuring stream, leafy green plants, and discreet shelter carry you miles away from the city in this sloping urban side yard. Seen here are the glossy leaves of Japanese holly fern (Cyrtomium falcatum) at lower right, pink blooms of hardy begonia (B. grandis), and feathery fronds of assorted wood ferns (Dryopteris).

way, being staggered with gaps between them like a giant picket fence. They also serve as a supersized canvas for catching and displaying the sunrays that slant down into the garden.

Finally, Jay uses plants to catch light. Variegated foliage and warm tones light up the dark shadows. Plants with translucent leaves glow during their brief time in the sun. As those rays move across the garden, highlighting different plants, the effect is ever-changing.

A seating area on the deck directly behind Jay's house overlooks the most colorful section of his woodland garden. All over the low, terraced slope that surrounds the seating area, he has planted out many coleus (Sole-nostemon) that he grew from cuttings in his greenhouse

Woolly thyme (Thymus pseudolanuginosus) flows among perennials and ornamental grasses, including mounds of blue oat grass (Helictotrichon sempervirens). A restrained palette of greens keeps this garden serene.

over the winter. They are scattered among the perennial variegated hostas, ferns, and sedges, adding splashes of crimson and lime green and peach. Retaining some space in his garden for these annuals gives Jay a chance to experiment with different color combinations and change the view from year to year; he enjoys this creative outlet.

Jay's garden looks larger than it is because he has blocked off views of the neighboring buildings and pulled the eye toward sculptures and other points of interest within it. But the hillside stream, the ponds, the pondside seating area, and the coleus-decorated woodland floor fit into about 1,300 square feet between his house and his neighbor's.

Maintenance is very easy, he says, with the main tasks being periodic filter pad cleaning, removing leaves from the ponds, and watering the woodland plants in dry weather. And of course, taking cuttings of the coleus in the fall, tending them over the winter, and planting them out in the spring.

Jay says he chose to make a woodland garden and include a water garden because both seemed to work with his piece of land. "The bottom line is to let your land speak to you," he recommends. "Before you do anything, just go out and sit in the middle of it. Feel when and from which direction the sun hits your skin. Feel how the wind blows. And listen to your garden. Listen to what it wants to become. It may surprise you, but self-fulfillment will surely follow and you'll garden with a smile on your face."

serenity in the shade

Woodland gardens are by nature subdued and serene. Designers of traditional Asian gardens have perfected serenity-promoting strategies like spreading gravel or groundcovers over large areas, limiting the flowers and colors, and carefully choosing the shapes of plants and rocks. A large colony of a single plant species lets our eyes travel calmly across a scene, soothing us without

demanding our focused attention. This can refresh our minds and free them to wander. Research has shown that passive enjoyment of natural scenery increases the brain's ability to focus, analyze, and learn.

Extensive plant colonies also add an air of maturity to a garden. You can use fast growers to achieve this effect, but you might have to work harder to keep them contained once they have filled their allotted territory. Another option is to use slower spreaders and grow them from seed, buy plugs (very small plants), or buy a few larger potted plants and manually divide and spread the plants each year until you have covered the area.

This urban woodland garden is at its heart a multi-textured tapestry of foliage. "The best thing about having less lawn is the enjoyment the neighbors and I get from a beautiful garden," says the homeowner, who designed, installed, and maintains it himself.

In a garden with limited colors and few or no flowers, texture and shape matter more. Notice and employ the craggy or smooth surface of rocks and tree trunks, and those with marbling or carved patterns or peeling bark, to add visual drama to your design. Choose path materials with an eye to their textural interest, or use them to add color. Garden art and sculpture can more easily take center stage in a woodland garden, whereas they might be out-competed by flowers in a livelier area. The shapes of leaves and the growth patterns of the plants also have greater visual impact here, so if you have a flair for combining textures and shapes, show off your skill in a shade garden.

A woodland garden with interesting textures in hardscape, rocks, art, and tree trunks has a beauty that endures throughout the year.

art in leaf

A garden given over primarily to foliage can be a powerful mood setter. The mood can be dark and unsettling or deeply reassuring, depending on your plant choices and your design. The mood can also vary by season.

You may feel there is not enough "flower power" in a shady setting. While it's true that woodland gardens won't usually accommodate flower-packed planting beds, it is definitely possible to design a shady space with visual punch. You can turn to annuals to add color, like Jay Sifford did in his North Carolina garden. Some perennials have variegated foliage as well. Even a subtly patterned plant can make a big visual impact if you plant it in masses, and if the plants aren't competing against a bright display of nearby flowers.

Shrubs are effective vehicles for adding color to a garden, because they grow to fill up more of the view. Choose shrubs with striking leaves, flowers, or berries; some may have all three. Shrubs native to woodland settings will be well adapted to living under and among trees, so it will be easier to keep them healthy.

Dark green leaves of hellebore (Helleborus) contrast dramatically with the delicate pastel flowers and divided leaves of fumewort (Pseudofumaria lutea).

Shady conditions will often prompt plants to develop large leaves so they can absorb more light. These large leaves attract notice because their shapes are so prominent and well defined. The list is long if you want to include large leaves in your woodland garden. Possibilities include hosta (*Hosta*), pigsqueak (*Bergenia*), false forget-me-not (*Brunnera*), foxglove (*Digitalis*), primrose (*Primula*), wild ginger (*Asarum*), and mayapple (*Podophyllum*). Serendipitously, many lacy-leaved plants grow well in shade, and these make a fine foil for the bold-leaved plants. Ferns, bleeding hearts (*Dicentra*) and their wild relatives, fumewort (*Pseudofumaria lutea*), goatsbeard

The woodland gardener can select from among a variety of foliage colors including reds, bronzes, golds, blues, silvers, and different variegated markings. To make a refined combination, pair colored foliage with flowers of a similar hue or in the same color family (gold and cream, for instance). For a more dramatic look, combine colors that are very different from each other or come from opposite sides of the color wheel (orange and blue, purple and yellow). In the shade, pastel colors show up better than bold ones, so choose white, pale yellow, pale pink, silver, and light blue to get the most visual contrast. If you find all these color choices overwhelming, you can limit your color scheme or choose a few signature plants to tie your garden together.

featuring trees

Trees form walls and ceilings that can shape the space in your garden. Tree islands, groves, and clearings are larger landscape elements that allow opportunities for diverse planting and make a powerful visual impact.

The area under and around a tree offers an array of sunny and shady sites suitable for diverse and vertically layered planting. Your trees can thrive if you convert the lawn around them to well-chosen ground-layer plants. Even under one tree, it's possible to create a plant community that sustains its own health, requiring less support from you.

Tree islands are useful large-scale design elements that can screen part of the view, adding mystery and privacy or simply drawing attention to what remains visible. They also create a view, filling up more of your field of vision. Situated in a mown lawn, they offer an easily maintained site for ground-layer plants that spread. You can use one or more tree islands to shrink your lawn to a wide path that wanders between the plantings, and this might give you the best of both worlds: the visual delight of a lawn and the space to walk barefoot on it, plus more room

(*Aruncus dioicus*), false spirea (*Astilbe* ×*arendsii*), and many more fall into this category.

Grassy plants provide yet another contrasting shape. Shade-adapted grassy plants include many sedges (*Carex*), a populous and diverse genus of grass-like plants of different heights, from the 6-inch oak sedge (*C. pensylvanica*) to the 3-foot fringed sedge (*C. crinita*); different blade widths, from the diminutive and fine-bladed bristleleaf sedge (*C. eburnea*) to the inch-wide blades of silver sedge (*C. platyphylla*); and with various seedheads, from the ornamental spiked nuts of gray's sedge (*C. grayi*) to the dangly pods of drooping sedge (*C. pendula*).

given to planted areas. A wide lawn path around a tree island makes an enticing play area for children too.

You can use a tree island to reduce some of your workload, by letting nature take care of it for you. Rather than removing fallen leaves from your lawn and carting them away, rake them into your tree island, where they will decompose into nutritious soil to feed your tree and its understory plants. This is healthier for your tree than having a lawn growing under it.

However, be aware that shrinking your lawn area with tree islands may not reduce your workload if it increases the amount of edges that you have to maintain. Give thought to the length of new edge you are creating, and to how you plan to maintain it. In general, minimizing your total edge length and using straighter, simpler edges will reduce your maintenance work, as will keeping edging and paving lower than the lawn to eliminate the need for a second pass with a trimmer.

If you have more than one tree growing in your lawn, you might design a larger island to incorporate multiple trees, making a grove rather than separate islands around each tree. With numerous small islands, you'll be running an obstacle course every time you mow, not to mention any trimming you may want to do around the edges of the islands. A grove keeps edge length to a minimum and creates opportunities to add different plants, allowing more space for understory trees and shrubs, as well as the possibility of a densely shaded interior area for woodland species. It also gives your trees a larger root zone with the conditions they prefer and is more wind-resistant than a single tree.

Make a path to give people access to the interior of your grove; the changes in light intensity and openness will make the landscape feel more dynamic and will enrich their experience of your garden.

A grove can be a large and powerful landscape feature, with more impact than an individual tree. It can be limbed up to create a leafy ceiling above the pillars of

the trunks, evoking a temple or cathedral and fostering a reverent mood. For a striking effect, plant (or make an island bed around) several trees of the same species and tie them together by underplanting the entire grove with one living carpet. If the plants are chosen with an eye for their colors and textures, this feature can shine.

Consider creating at least one clearing in your shade garden. Clearings add crucial human habitat to a wooded landscape. On emerging from under the tree canopy, we respond with enthusiasm to a glimpse of the sky. Natural clearings are home to many kinds of meadows, and this would make a logical place for a low-care grassy area. It is also the most sensible place for a lawn if you have a lot of trees around; however, a meadow's less frequent demands might better preserve the serenity of the surrounding garden.

As with groves and tree islands, including a clearing boosts both the variety of plants you can grow and the variety of light and shade in your garden. This creates excitement and augments the sensory power of the garden. For maximum effect, site a bench or other seat in or at the edge of a clearing, where the diverse environments and plants are most visible; it will likely possess the best views in your shady garden.

---

*top: Deadnettle (*Lamium maculatum *'White Nancy' and L. m. 'Silver Beacon') swirls around mounds of hostas and mature spruces (*Picea*) at West of the Lake Gardens in Manitowoc, Wisconsin.*

*bottom: Shielding an outdoor seating area from the street are two square gardens with matching groves of birches (*Betula*). Each is carpeted with a different groundcover, catmint (*Nepeta*) in the foreground and false spirea (*Astilbe ×arendsii*) in the back, for an effect that is elegant in every season.*

meadow and
prairie gardens

Indiangrass (Sorghastrum nutans) demonstrates that grass inflorescences can be as lovely as any flower.

grasses have been rediscovered, their airy structures unleashed in new meadow and prairie gardens, after a century of being relegated to lawns and weedy fields. They deserve the appreciation we are now showing them for their ability to embody a breeze, catch light, soften the view, and for their showiness in late summer and early autumn, when most traditional perennials have faded.

Different types of grasses fit different climates and soil conditions. In wet places and coastal zones, grasses are key components of low marsh and dune landscapes. In central North America, tallgrass prairies above head height once covered miles and miles of land where woodlands were kept back by fire or inadequate precipitation. Drier western and southwestern areas support shortgrass prairies with occasional shrubs. Specialized grasses also thrive in forest clearings, riverside bluffs, and many other peculiar geographies. Though they may not be the plants you notice first, grasses are what give prairies, meadows, and marshes their unique character. They (or sedges, or rushes, or sometimes ferns) form a "fabric" with various companion plants woven through it.

*A stunning swath of pink muhly grass (**Muhlenbergia capillaris**) flowers in a front yard garden in California. For gardeners north of zone 6, a similar, shorter option is purple love grass (**Eragrostis spectabilis**).*

Not only do they add structure and life above the ground, grasses also build structure and enable life underground. This is how deep, fertile soils, once home to tallgrass prairies and still being mined today, were created. The fibrous netlike roots of grasses (unless they are curtailed by frequent mowing) weave through the soil among the less dense roots of flowering and woody plants, sewing them together with a thick web and filling the available soil. Including a substantial portion of grasses in your plant community will help keep weeds at bay.

The liberal inclusion of shier grasses can bring subtle organization to a garden, while the powerful presence of bolder grasses infuses an area with life and personality. Whether sited in sun or shade, sheltered or exposed, grasses are conduits of light and wind. If you think you love your lawn, wait till you meet her wild sisters.

dinner in the prairie

Tom Haigh and Karen Canon are both dedicated cyclists who enjoy spending time outdoors but cannot afford to spend a lot of time gardening. They swim, eat, and cook outside when they can, and they frequently entertain their adult children and other guests in their suburban backyard.

Their house has a walkout lower level that opens onto a steeply sloping backyard. When the big back deck that they had lived with for years finally rotted away, they hired a landscaper to create several paved terraces linked by short series of steps. This made a durable, functional hardscape with easier access to the swimming pool. Hauled-in boulders were partly buried in the steep slopes to retain and beautify them. The planting areas were dressed with topsoil and mulched with wood chips.

Their garden was ready to be planted, but Tom and Karen weren't sure what to plant, and they didn't have much money left over for the plants. While they considered their next step, the rains washed much of their new soil and mulch down onto their new patios. They needed plants that would establish quickly and hold the steep slopes against erosion.

Over a delicious dinner in their boulder-dominated landscape one evening, I suggested they could make an inexpensive prairie garden using small potted seedlings of native grasses and flowers, with a few judiciously placed larger pots of non-native groundcovers like creeping thyme and creeping phlox to fill in the understory and address their erosion issues more quickly.

They agreed, I drew up a design for this prairie-style garden, and we planted the first batch of plants soon after. Their plants came from local growers, mainly as 4-inch pots and plugs, which are very small seedlings sold in flats. Their small sizes meant they were easier to plant and took off quickly. (If you don't have a native plant grower near you, you might find a specialist nursery that can sell you plugs, for which shipping would not be cost-prohibitive.)

Just a year after planting, the erosion of mulch and soil onto their terraces had nearly stopped, and after several years their slope was blanketed with a happy mix of grasses and flowers. On the steeper parts of the slope and along the fence, masses of deep-rooted little bluestem (*Schizachyrium scoparium*) hold the soil against erosion and act as a barrier to unwanted plants creeping in from the neighbor's yard. In front of the grasses, purple coneflowers (*Echinacea purpurea*), orange-blooming butterflyweed (*Asclepias tuberosa*), and grayheaded coneflowers (*Ratibida pinnata*) attired in butter-yellow sashay down the slope, with occasional supportive clusters of little bluestem. The flowers stand out vividly against the blue-green blades of the grasses. An understory of lower plants including coreopsis (*C. verticillata* 'Moonbeam'), winecups (*Callirhoe involucrata*), and creeping phlox (*P. subulata* 'Blue

*top: Encircling a terrace in this sloping backyard, a four-year-old prairie-style garden in Minnesota makes a lively backdrop through the seasons. The showy blossoms of purple coneflower (*Echinacea purpurea) attract butterflies and people.*

bottom: View of the terrace and slope—with boulders— before the garden was planted.

Shorter plants, includ-
ing lavender wild petunia
(Ruellia humilis), *flank the
rock staircase.*

*A prairie undergoes dramatic
changes over the course of the
year, and a prairie-style garden, even a small one, brings
this same dynamism into
your landscape. Here, little
bluestem (Schizachyrium
scoparium) reaches its peak
color in late fall, when most
other perennials have dried
or died back.*

Emerald') covers the ground densely, contributing color, texture, nectar, shelter, and support. Flocks of red admiral and monarch butterflies add life to the scene with their fluttering and swooping. Ranged along the bottom of the slope, several massive, sculptural clumps of prairie dock (*Silphium terebinthinaceum*) provide dramatic structure. Their deep, thirsty roots ensure that any runoff that might make it past the other plants is absorbed before it reaches the pavement.

Along the rock staircase up to their back gate, we mingled a variety of short native plants, including the early-flowering and charismatic prairie smoke (*Geum triflorum*); coralbells (*Heuchera americana*), with its softly glowing flowers and tidy mounds of leaves; junegrass (*Koeleria macrantha*) for its deep root network and spring showiness; the silvery creeping pussytoes (*Antennaria neglecta*); and blue-flowered harebell (*Campanula rotundifolia*) and flax (*Linum lewisii*). All these plants self-sow in the rock crevices and bare places, filling every available niche. Across the staircase from the prairie plants, a blanket of creeping thyme (*Thymus serpyllum*) spreads down the slope, and stiff stalks of native leadplant (*Amorpha canescens*) raise iridescent purple flowers above the purple-pink blooms of the thyme.

Maintenance involves periodically wandering through the garden and pulling a few weeds—mainly tree seedlings and weeds that creep or blow in from neighboring yards. Plants are watered only during times of unusual drought. Early every spring, Tom and Karen cut down the dead grasses and flowers to make way for the coming year's show.

How often do they watch that show? Tom says they are out in the garden "every late afternoon and evening that it's not raining, from May through September." His favorite thing about the garden is its seasonal progression, from the earliest low-blooming phlox to the last hurrah of the asters. And Karen's? "It just comes up by itself with almost no effort from us."

prairie hotbed

Susan Damon adores native plants and backyard bird watching. She has transformed her urban yard into a wildlife haven with native shrubs that shelter and feed many songbirds, native flowers that host assorted butterflies and other nectar lovers, and a rich mix of ground-layer plants native to prairies and woodlands.

Susan is the self-proclaimed "head gardener" of the household, and her husband, Paul, a landscape architect and landscape painter, was "head designer." They both enjoy the haven that their yard now provides for people as well as for wildlife. Their house is located on a busy corner, with cars and buses passing by all day and much of the night. However they can find peace, comfort, and endless entertainment relaxing in their sheltered seating area, while around them various birds go about the business of gathering food, building nests, and raising young.

Susan and Paul's front boulevard—a 6- by 80-foot strip of land between the street and the sidewalk—displays a profusion of flowers supported by an understory of lower grasses and herbs. The plants take turns providing a show as the seasons pass, so the boulevard looks dramatically different over the course of a year.

Despite the height restrictions imposed on the garden by a city ordinance, the mix of plants is diverse, with over 40 species knit together in a three-dimensional display. In the center of the boulevard, plants can be somewhat taller; such flowers and grasses include little bluestem (*Schizachyrium scoparium*), golden alexanders (*Zizia aurea*), several species of milkweed (*Asclepias*) and coreopsis, and Virginia spiderwort (*Tradescantia virginiana*). In the understory, low sedums, chives (*Allium schoenoprasum*), spearmint (*Mentha spicata*), and culinary oregano (*Origanum vulgare*) join low natives such as oak sedge (*Carex pensylvanica*), northern bedstraw (*Galium boreale*), junegrass (*Koeleria macrantha*), and bigleaf aster (*Eurybia macrophylla*), filling the ground and keeping out weeds.

Plant height is even more strictly limited near the street corner, where a rich blend of at least a dozen species, including partridge pea (*Chamaecrista fasciculata*), hairy wood mint (*Blephilia hirsuta*), path rush (*Juncus tenuis*), wild petunia (*Ruellia humilis*), and hoary vervain (*Verbena stricta*), makes a thick, knee-high tapestry of color. Boulevard height and species restrictions are set locally; check with your city to find out what restrictions might apply to your own boulevard garden.

Susan says additional plants that self-sow into the boulevard are mainly volunteers from her garden above, and she digs out or cuts down the ones that don't meet the height restriction. Otherwise maintenance is low due to the diversity of well-adapted plants she has chosen. "I don't ever water established plants and don't do much weeding either," she says. "Once the plantings establish good cover, there aren't many weeds."

However, gardening on an urban boulevard does pose challenges, which is why author Lauren Springer Ogden coined the term "hellstrip" to describe these scraps of land. This garden is plagued by heat and dryness in summer, piled snow and road salt in winter, and heavy machinery year-round. But when a schoolbus drives across it, or a street maintenance vehicle tears up an area, Susan matter-of-factly renews it with the abundant seedlings produced by the well-adapted plants in other parts of her yard. Other maintenance involves cutting back prairie

sage and a few others to keep them compact. She leaves the dead plants standing through the winter to feed the birds and let beneficial insects overwinter in the stalks and dried foliage. In early spring, she cuts back the entire boulevard manually, using loppers and pruners.

In addition to bringing in wildlife and making their lawnmower obsolete, one of the biggest benefits of converting their lawn to a four-season garden has been the wealth of material it now provides for photographing the plants and the multitude of butterflies, bugs, and birds. Susan regularly presents slideshows, using her photos to illustrate the rewards of living closer to plants and animals. "I have taken thousands of garden photos," she says. "Could you imagine taking thousands of lawn photos?"

shockingly simple meadow garden

Grass aficionados salivate at the mention of our native prairie dropseed (*Sporobolus heterolepis*), a charismatic and elegant grass with a long list of desirable traits: mounding habit, bright green foliage, slender stem with an airy seedhead, and the mild, warm aroma of freshly popped popcorn. Spread that grass over an entire meadow, and you will have a landscape to swoon over. Add a few judicious ornamental plants (in this case, native flowers and bulbs), and really there is no leaving once a person has stepped into such a place.

A dropseed meadow was installed at Olbrich Botanical Gardens in Madison, Wisconsin, in 2009, replacing a Kentucky bluegrass lawn and covering an area of roughly 70 by 40 feet. Packed gravel paths are wide enough that the grasses can arch gracefully out onto them. An intimate seating area beckons from one corner, backed by a protective hedge of shrubs and taller grasses that hold in the delicious dropseed scent. Against their dark green foliage, the seedheads of the grasses dance and tremble like light personified.

Large drifts of plants like this appeal to us for the sheer exuberance of having so much, and yet their simplicity can also relax us. That is one reason why many people love to look at a lawn, and why farm fields with their patchwork of monocultures have inspired poetic admiration for centuries. Even if an individual plant is not showy or interesting, a mass of it can be thrilling.

Given how important biodiversity is to balancing populations in a landscape and boosting our Earth's ability to support life, you may be thinking that we should all add as many different plants to our gardens as we can. Although biodiversity has many benefits and is crucial for returning life to our landscapes, there is also a place for creating some areas with simpler landscapes—even monocultures—that give people pleasant places to spend time outside.

There is also an argument to be made for replacing intensively maintained monocultures like lawns with single-species (or nearly) stands of uncut perennials or grasses. Large drifts of one kind of plant are relatively easy to maintain, especially for a new gardener or a very busy person who wants to have a garden. They make less demanding solutions for out-of-the-way areas, future garden spaces, and other parts of the garden that you can't spend much time on. Where you just want an easy temporary—or permanent—substitute for a lawn, a low-care mass of another plant can be an eco-friendly (environmentally sound and sustainable) alternative.

Autumn brings yet another revolution of color and pattern in the prairie boulevard, with seedheads of junegrass (Koeleria macrantha) and winsome blooms of heart-leaf aster (Symphyotrichum cordifolium).

This dropseed meadow, which looks kind of like a tall lawn, supports significantly more life. First, its height allows little creatures to safely crawl or hop or slither through it, maybe even to live there. Second, it attracts insects that eat the grass leaves, and birds that eat those insects and the grass seeds. (Being regionally native helps; a non-native ornamental grass might not be palatable to local insects that have not evolved to bypass its specific chemical constituents.) Third, it is part of a larger diverse landscape, and it allows safe passage between different parts of that landscape rather than cutting off movement like a shorn lawn would. So while this meadow garden may not have the habitat value of a woodland or prairie,

At Olbrich Botanical Gardens, a meadow of prairie dropseed (Sporobolus heterolepis) flows out from a sheltered seating area. On the right are two well-chosen companion plants, white-flowered gaura (G. lindheimeri) and Chinese fountain grass (Pennisetum alopecuroides 'Hameln').

it offers shelter, food, and safe passage to many more creatures than a lawn would support, and it may be an appealing alternative for those who love the simple, uniform look of a lawn.

As for maintenance, every spring the meadow is cut down, the clippings taken away and composted, and a layer of leaf mulch added to keep weeds down. Only light, manual spot-weeding is needed every now and then, and these regionally adapted grasses thrive with no supplemental water.

Feel like trying it? Many other grasses could be used to create equally stunning and unique (and low-care) gardens. Just choose a species that grows well in your site's conditions, perhaps add a few ornamental plants for contrast, and you'll soon be relaxing and admiring your own shockingly simple meadow garden.

flower-powered prairies

After centuries of plowing them under to make farms and towns and roads and shopping centers, original prairies are extremely rare in our modern landscape. However, their diversity and drama have earned them many ardent supporters. The research of prairie ecologists, the dedication of plant growers, and the skill of restorationists have made it possible for the average homeowner to establish a successful, authentic (meaning ecologically correct) prairie garden. Ensuring that the prairie will have a long, healthy life will require specialized knowledge and several years of dedicated care; however, a determined novice armed with an informative seed catalog from a reliable grower can do it fairly inexpensively.

In general, tallgrass prairies are well suited to areas of central North America with moister climates and clay-rich soils. In sandy or shallow soils, and in drier western, southwestern, and intermountain climates, shortgrass prairies grow naturally and are usually a better option. Wet prairies are adapted for low-lying areas and where the water table is high or there is seasonal standing water. Wet-prairie plants can also be used in rain gardens, shorelines, swales, biofilter plantings, and other landscape strategies for managing urban and suburban runoff.

For an authentic prairie, it is important to choose locally native plants, grown from the seeds of plants that

Diane Hilscher's custom seed blend, a 50/50 mix of regionally native grasses and flowers, gives this front yard tallgrass prairie eye-popping color, while creating a healthy blend of root structures for thick coverage and weed resistance.

naturally occur within a certain distance of your property. These regional ecotypes are (broadly speaking) the plants that have evolved alongside your local wildlife, including local insects that form the basis of the food chain as well as local soil microbes that convert waste materials into nutrients that feed your plants. They have also evolved to take advantage of your local climate and will generally emerge, bloom, and set seed at the most effective time of year. Plants of the same species that come from other parts of the continent may not be able to reproduce in your garden, or to provide nectar when the pollinators need it most, or to build many of the other relationships that power a healthy ecological community.

Though you may be tempted to pack your prairie with flowers, half or more of the individual plants should be grasses if your prairie is to have a long life. Grass roots fill the soil between the sparser roots of the flowers, so an established prairie with a good base of grasses can better resist invasion by shrubs and trees as well as wind-blown weeds. Some prairie flowers with scanty base foliage (such as *Liatris* and most *Asclepias* species) also show better and withstand breaking or mashing by heavy rains if they are physically supported by surrounding grasses.

Native prairies typically contain 70 to 90 percent grass species. To provide more flower power, you could follow the lead of Minnesota-based landscape architect and ecologist Diane Hilscher, who uses a custom mix of 50 percent flowers and 50 percent grasses to ensure a healthy prairie with an adequate proportion of grass, but with more flowers than you might find in a natural prairie.

Reputable growers will list the origin of their seeds or plants in their catalogs, and most will be eager to supply you with instructions for establishing a prairie and maintaining it. It is becoming easier to find companies that specialize in planned burns, weed removal, and other prairie maintenance strategies, and they can be hired to make an annual or every-few-years visit to keep on top of any potential problems.

Once they are established, prairies make a waterwise, mainly self-sustaining landscape that can replace extensive lawns, old fields, roadsides, parks, and other land that is not used for ball games or similar recreational activities. Transitioning to a less intensively maintained prairie landscape will save money, water, and work. Your prairie will also reward you with wildlife habitat, year-round beauty, and many seasons of exploring, watching bugs and birds, taking photos, and imagining the splendid "amber waves" that once rolled across miles of our continent's interior.

bulb-injected meadows

In another part of Olbrich Botanical Gardens, a ten-year-old meadow spreads under scattered crabapple (*Malus*) and redbud (*Cercis canadensis*) trees. Made of mixed clumping fescues, including chewing's (*Festuca rubra* subsp. *fallax*), sheep (*F. ovina*), and hard (*F. brevipila*) fescues, this meadow also replaced a Kentucky bluegrass lawn and is intended to demonstrate to homeowners how they can have a low-care, low-growing area with minimal ecological impact and maximum beauty.

The turf was killed in fall 1999 and allowed to decompose all winter. In spring it was run across with a mechanical dethatcher, then a seed mix was sown. In autumn 2000, after the fescues had begun to settle in, 13,000 minor bulbs (short species with smaller flowers) were planted throughout the meadow. They included diminutive forms of ornamental onion (*Allium*), windflower (*Anemone*), crocus (*Crocus*), fritillary (*Fritillaria*), summer snowflake (*Leucojum*), squill (*Scilla*), and species tulips (*Tulipa*). Thousands more were added each fall for the next several years, and springs now shimmer with color as the flowers come and go, some lasting only a week. By summer, the bulbs have subsided, and fescues and perennials take over.

The fescue meadow at Olbrich spreads under spring-flowering trees.

When the flowering trees bloom in concert above the meadow, visitors to the garden are awed by its glory, says director Jeff Epping, who masterminded this meadow as well as the dropseed meadow described earlier. For a small initial investment, most of them could probably create the same visual splendor at home, where their lawn is now.

Not only would a meadow like this be more beautiful to most of us, but it would also be easier and less costly to care for than picture-perfect turf. This meadow is cut twice a year—once in midsummer after the bulb foliage

has browned and the fescues have formed seedheads, and again in late fall to make way for next spring's flowers. The clippings are removed to keep fertility low, which the fescues prefer and which also keeps the area from attracting many weeds. For that same reason, fertilizing would be counterproductive. The meadow was not watered after the first two years, as fescues prefer dry soil, and this too keeps the weeds down.

Once a year any bare spots are overseeded. If the fescue blend included creeping fescues, this would probably not be necessary as they would "self-repair" by filling any bare spots. Jeff recommends that area meadow gardeners use the "Care-free" fescue blend (which includes both creeping and clumping fescues) from Olds Seed Solutions, available in independent garden centers and hardware stores. This blend would work for gardeners through the northern and upper midwest regions; western and southwestern folks will have better luck with dry-adapted grasses.

To keep its thousands of visitors from trampling the flowers, a stone path winds through the fescue meadow at Olbrich. Fescues can take heavy foot traffic, so a path would not be necessary at all in a home garden. However, for an easy path you could mow one and change its course every few years.

Jeff has made a similar fescue meadow at home in place of his front lawn. He mows it three times a year, does not give it any supplemental water, and hand weeds occasionally. It has seen traffic from two hundred people during a garden tour with no discernible damage; during the tour several people commented on its beauty and asked how he got that "combed look."

Imagine how peaceful and beautiful our neighborhoods could be (and how much water, money, time, and fuel we'd save) if we all grew low meadows rather than lawns. The sounds of nature could be heard again. The sweet breath of growing plants would infuse the air. In our free time, we could relax, surrounded by nature's glory.

Pink flower balls adorn an urban front meadow garden injected with ornamental onion (Allium giganteum 'Globemaster').

rain gardens

Undeveloped natural areas are living sponges that absorb stormwater, snowmelt, and flood waters into a system of soil, networks of roots, and permanent and temporary water bodies above and below the ground. Such natural areas cleanse the water and release it back into the air (through evaporation and transpiration), to fall again as precipitation. As we have covered more of the land with impervious surfaces, we have disrupted this natural water cycle. Runoff has fewer places to go, especially in our urban areas, where up to 90 percent of the surface area can be impervious.

Intensively managed lawns have a limited ability to absorb runoff. Their leaves are kept short, so they cannot photosynthesize enough to grow and support extensive root systems, and their roots don't need to develop if they are watered frequently and shallowly. Urban and suburban lawns that were compacted during development may soak up only a fraction of the runoff that lawns with deeper soils could. Where you need a more absorbent landscape, rain gardens are an easy and effective solution.

Gently shaping the earth can have a big impact on how water flows and where it collects. A rain garden can move the runoff from your roof or pavement into your soil before it creates problems for you and your neighbors. The cheapest and easiest solution to runoff is an eco-friendly one too: slow it down, spread it out, and absorb it into the soil, letting natural processes manage it without any further cost or effort on your part.

Rain garden plants: working for you, and beautiful too. Cardinal flower (Lobelia cardinalis) sizzles among seedpods of swamp milkweed (Asclepias incarnata), and behind, the purple haze of joe pye weed (Eupatorium purpureum).

*A rain garden in a sloping lawn between two houses intercepts runoff before it reaches the street. Designed for maximum foliage appeal, it holds drifts of tall grasses, ferns, variegated solomon's seal (*Polygonatum odoratum var. thunbergii 'Variegatum'*), and low dwarf crested iris (*I. cristata*).*

Whether they are barely noticeable shallow basins, wide or narrow channels, or deep bowls in the land, rain gardens have a flat and level bottom that slows runoff and spreads it out, allowing more water to soak into the soil more quickly. But soil is just one of their strategies; the other is roots. As the plants in a rain garden grow, they fill the soil with a web of their roots, and this root network becomes more adept at soaking up water every year.

It may seem counterintuitive, but rainwater is especially beneficial for gardens in areas where rain is most scarce. Rainwater, being slightly acidic, is more suitable than tapwater for most plants, and dry-climate soils can be sensitive to a buildup of salts from frequent, quickly evaporated irrigation with municipal water. Plus rainwater is free. In a dry climate, you can create a passive irrigation system by making all your planting beds slightly sunken with flat bottoms, like little rain gardens, with paths and paved areas slightly raised to drain water into the beds.

To make a simple rain garden, dig a low area and pile the dug-up soil or sod on the downhill side to form a basin. Though in certain cases you may want a professionally engineered, foolproof rain garden, the average non-engineer can make an effective one in soil that drains well. (To test this, dig a hole and fill it with water, then watch how long it takes to empty.) Your rain garden can be any depth, but it need not be deeper than 6 inches. The key is to make the bottom flat and level, so water will spread out and soak into every part of it. To prevent breeding mosquitoes and black flies, make sure that standing water drains away within a few days. You can adjust this by installing an overflow pipe or digging an overflow channel, to drain water out of your rain garden once it reaches a certain depth.

Now for the fun part: the plants. Because they will get more water than other parts of your garden, you can try all sorts of interesting wet-adapted plants—gorgeous tall flowers, shrubs, and grasses that grow in wet prairies and natural shorelines. These may attract dragonflies that live in nearby water bodies. Ferns, sedges, and woodland wildflowers do well in the understory or if the garden is shaded. The drier microclimate around the higher sides of the rain garden gives you a chance to grow different plants that like those conditions, so you can end up with an exciting variety of plants in a small space. Once their roots are established, nature can supply much or all of the water they need. Oh yes, and they take care of your runoff for you too.

functional and floriferous

Kathy Smith's front garden blooms among the well-kept lawns of her suburban neighborhood. Lawnless except for a narrow strip of turf around two sides, it includes a large rain garden sited in a naturally low area near the front edge of the yard. Shallow channels carry roof runoff from her two drainspouts past herbs, drifts of perennial flowers, and a fruit tree. The channels lead into the rain garden, home to an exuberant assembly of tall grasses and moisture-loving native flowers.

A low berm on the street side of the rain garden is planted with tall grasses and perennials emerging from a carpet of mat-forming shrubs. The feather reed grasses (*Calamagrostis ×acutiflora* 'Karl Foerster') provide a beautiful backdrop for Kathy's flowers, and their height ensures that plants rather than buildings and cars fill most of the views from her windows, bringing her garden into the house.

The front garden was designed by Paula Westmoreland of Ecological Gardens in Minneapolis. In addition to the rain garden, it includes a row of edible plants and an herb spiral. Roses grow companionably among the tall grasses on the berm, and beyond it, a strip of turfgrass separates the garden from the street. Showy little bluestem (*Schizachyrium scoparium* 'Carousel'), catmint (*Nepeta*), and joe pye weed range alongside the driveway where they are most visible, and bright masses of yarrow (*Achillea* 'Moonshine'), oxeye (*Heliopsis* 'Tuscan Sun'), spiked speedwell (*Veronica spicata* 'Purpleicious'), and other perennials contribute color.

Kathy says her neighbors have been "curious and supportive" about the new garden. "We get lots of compliments about how pretty it is to look at now." It works too, soaking up runoff from their roof before it reaches the street, using that water to grow ornamental blooms and plumes rather than sending it into the city storm sewer system. Best of all, this garden is only two years

*top: Flag iris (*I. versicolor*), a showy native, blooms in the wettest part of this front yard rain garden, alongside the dangly seedheads of fringed sedge (*Carex crinita*) and the flat-topped inflorescences of golden alexanders (*Zizia aurea*).*

bottom: A shallow channel carries roof runoff to the rain garden, where it is absorbed into soil and roots.

Appealing throughout the growing season, this rain garden reaches its height of glory in late summer, when purple cone-flower (Echinacea purpurea), cardinal flower (Lobelia cardinalis), feather reed grass (Calamagrostis ×acutiflora 'Karl Foerster'), and joe pye weed (Eupatorium purpureum) mingle their tall and colorful heads.

The colors and textures of these rain garden plants contrast vividly with traditional lawns, where nothing moves and no changes mark the passing of the seasons.

old, and it will become even more lush, colorful, and absorbent every year.

The garden is thickly mulched to keep down weeds while the permanent plants establish. Though some weeds still find their way into the bare places, the ornamental grasses and perennials will cover most of the ground within a few years. Other than an annual cutting back, which Kathy does in early spring so the standing stalks can add winter interest, most of the plants need no particular attention to thrive. Those that are sited in and around the rain garden need no supplemental watering; neither do the drought-tolerant natives and herbs, nor the deep-rooted ornamental grasses.

"Actually the trickiest part is keeping the grass border in the front looking good," says Kathy. To be fair, her answer reflects more of a personal preference than the difference in care needed by lawns versus perennial gardens. She says she wanted to make a garden because she never was good at growing a lawn, and it was boring, whereas she loves being out in her garden. She spends pleasurable hours in direct contact with her plants, snipping dead blooms off the larger flowers, and every summer she cuts down the yarrow which "goes wild and turns brown" after it has finished blooming. It's not just that her efforts pay off by making the garden extra showy. "I find dead-heading very therapeutic," she admits. Many gardeners can empathize.

channeling runoff

Runoff comes not only from the roof but also from the surrounding landscape. In a hilly neighborhood, water flows across roads and lawns, and properties that are located further downhill get a larger amount of water moving across their landscapes and past their houses. Runoff can erode sloping gardens and lawns, wash away soil and plants, and pool next to buildings and in low areas.

Rain gardens can be a beautiful and surprisingly powerful tool to counter extreme surges of runoff. This linear garden, containing two rain gardens and a swale, flows down a large hill and extends over 150 feet. Its edges curve in and out to break up the movement of water and disperse it in different directions. It spans an entire side of a large suburban lot, from the street above to a pond below. The owner, Pratibha Gupta, built the pond years before putting in the rain garden. After rainstorms and the spring snowmelt, "the runaway water and silt would make cleaning the pond a nightmare," she recalls. "Building the garden has solved this problem."

Designed by Paula Westmoreland and installed by Ecological Gardens, this garden uses several innovative techniques that work together to handle the enormous quantity of runoff the property receives. At the street, the curb is cut to let water flow down the steep slope, where it enters the large upper rain garden. Boulders and piles of smaller rocks help to slow and break up the flow of water as it enters, and they also trap silt, cleaning the water.

Because the slope is so steep, it can be very dry between rain events, so the plants must tolerate both drought and flood. As this garden is visible from the street and surrounding properties, it was desirable for the plants to also be ornamental. Paula anchored this upper rain garden with arctic blue willow (*Salix purpurea* 'Nana'), dappled willow (*S. integra* 'Hakuro-nishiki'), and elderberry (*Sambucus*) shrubs. The willows have attractive

The underlying structure of this garden is clearly visible shortly after installation and planting. The garden uses upper and lower rain gardens connected by a grassy swale to slow, absorb, and filter stormwater runoff from a hilly suburban neighborhood.

Three years later, the garden has filled out and effectively absorbs powerful surges of stormwater runoff. Thirsty shrubs grow at the top of the garden, including elder-berry (Sambucus) in the foreground and the creamy leaves of dappled willow (Salix integra 'Hakuro-nishiki') behind it.

Spring Blossoms, *a clay sculpture installation by Pratibha Gupta, stands on a grassy knoll in her rain garden.*

foliage and are early to leaf out in spring, the elderber-
ries have striking star-shaped arrays of leaves and produce
large white composite blossoms followed by clusters of
berries, and all are fast growers that become established
quickly, helping to take up moisture and hold the slope.
Among the shrubs she placed deep-rooted native prairie
grasses including little bluestem (*Schizachyrium scoparium*)
and indiangrass *(Sorghastrum nutans)*. The low berms
surrounding the rain garden are planted with perennial
flowers and groundcovers.

As water makes its way downhill through this upper
rain garden, the main channel divides into smaller channels to flow around several islands. Dividing the flow
weakens the water's destructive power. Thick tufts of tall
grass in its path force the water to meander, slowing it
further so that more of it can be absorbed. The islands
also provide niches for art and plants that enjoy drier
conditions.

At the mouth of the upper rain garden, water spills
over a waterfall; strategically placed rocks at its base slow
and direct the water into a grass swale with an island in
the middle. From the swale, water flows into a second
rain garden with more islands. The ground is flatter here
at the base of the slope, allowing the water to spread out
and soak into every part of the rain garden.

This multi-level linear garden took some time to become established. Several large rainstorms washed away
some of the small plants before they could develop roots
strong enough to withstand the surges of runoff. "The
first year was difficult," Pratibha admits. "Once the plants
and grasses got established, the garden worked like a
charm. My yard does not flood any more. It has reduced
my maintenance a lot."

After its fourth season, the garden still needs some
weeding. Time and effort for maintenance will decrease
every year as the plants continue to spread across the surface and into the soil, covering bare ground and growing
deeper, more absorbent root networks.

Pratibha is a painter, sculptor, and potter, and she uses
the garden to showcase some of her creations, placing
them on the islands to keep them dry. The delicate heads
of the grasses show up well against their solid tan and
red-brown forms. "Building this garden became a project
that I could use my talents for," she says. But to her the
best part of the garden is the living creatures it brings:
the flowers, butterflies, and bumble bees.

natural rain drinkers

The 1,000-square-foot rain garden at the University of
Wisconsin-Madison Arboretum contains over 40 native
plant species. It is a part of the four-acre Wisconsin
Native Plant Garden that surrounds the Visitor Center, a
large collection of smaller gardens that aims to demonstrate to the public how native plants and natural communities can be used to make functional, beautiful home
landscapes.

The rain garden was created by digging out a basin and
partly refilling it with a load of composted leaves, which
kept fertility high and generated good growth when
the plants were young. Roof runoff and air conditioner
condensate flow into the garden from pipes built into the
rock wall above it. It also receives water shed by about
1,200 square feet of higher ground around it. The garden
generally drains almost completely within a day or two after a rainstorm, though it may have standing water during
summers with heavy rain and during winters when it rains
on frozen soils. On the rare occasions when the standing
water gets deeper than 12 inches, an overflow pipe directs
it out of the garden and into the prairie beyond.

The garden's outer slope is covered with the running
low groundcover Canada anemone (*A. canadensis*). Its
large, lobed leaves wither to a crispy dark brown if it gets
too dry, but it will renew its foliage after a rain. Taller
grasses and flowers emerge from this living carpet. Jewelweed (*Impatiens capensis*), a self-sowing annual native to

moist woodlands, has volunteered in this garden and been welcomed; it attracts hummingbirds, bees, and moths.

The interior basin is filled with plants that enjoy wetter conditions. In the center is a large patch of bluejoint grass (*Calamagrostis canadensis*) interspersed with several taller plants. All are native to wetlands, but once established they have not needed supplemental water. In hot, dry weather the building's air conditioner runs more and produces more condensate to water the garden, and this has proven to supply enough water for even the handsome great bulrush.

Rain garden maintenance involves some hand weeding of non-native or too-aggressive species that self-sow into it. It is also burned every few years. This kills off unwanted non-native plants, most of which do not have the deep roots that allow the fire-adapted natives to regenerate after burning. Another reason for burning is to renew fertility by converting some dead plant matter to carbon-rich ash. For home gardens located in municipalities where burning is prohibited, the arboretum's native plant specialists recommend cutting and removing old plant matter in early spring, after leaving the stalks up for winter interest and wildlife habitat.

These photos were taken several months after a burn, in early fall, when the showiest plants are asters and grasses. Other species take the spotlight at different times of year. Whatever the season, this garden serves the mission of the arboretum well, demonstrating that rain gardens made with native plants are not only easy, but easy on the eye.

*In the rain garden at the UW-Madison Arboretum, swamp aster (*Symphyotrichum puniceum*) blooms "on a stick" like a natural topiary, emerging from a carpet of Canada anemone (A. canadensis), and purple New England aster (S. novae-angliae) and orange jewelweed (*Impatiens capensis*) grow among fine-leaved bluejoint grass (*Calamagrostis canadensis*). Wide-bladed shoots are cattail (*Typha*), an unwelcome volunteer which is being killed off by repeated cutting.*

top: Further down the slope, white-flowered heath aster (Symphyotrichum ericoides) blooms amid little bluestem (Schizachyrium scoparium), prairie dropseed (Sporobolus heterolepis), and sideoats grama (Bouteloua curtipendula) grasses.

bottom: Dominating the wettest part of the garden with its tall dark green stems and clusters of gold seeds is great bulrush (Schoenoplectus tabernaemontani), a wetland plant that tolerates periods of dry surface soil.

on the shady side

Rain gardens (and gardens in general) can absorb more runoff when they include trees and shrubs. These woody plants may not be showing obvious life or growth during every season, but they are still actively taking up some water whenever soil temperature is warm enough to allow root growth.

Roof runoff is absorbed by this shady garden bed alongside a garage. A perforated plastic hose extends from the downspout along the length of the planting bed (roughly 15 feet) and for several feet past the corner of the garage, where it empties into a perennial garden. The perforations let water trickle out of the hose all along its length, giving extra moisture to a couple of hophornbeams (*Ostrya virginiana*) and their understory of ferns and flowers.

This garden, designed by Diane Hilscher of Hilscher Design and Ecology, includes a host of plants for springtime bloom. Summer features the lacy textures of ostrich (*Matteuccia struthiopteris*) and maidenhair (*Adiantum pedatum*) ferns and false spirea (*Astilbe ×arendsii*), plus the colorful foliage and flowers of variegated yellow loosestrife (*Lysimachia punctata* 'Alexander') and variegated hostas. The low, vining groundcover periwinkle (*Vinca minor*) creeps among them all, covering any remaining bare ground; from this enclosed bed, it cannot escape to the nearby native woodland, where it might outcompete native ground-layer plants.

Before the perforated drainage hose was added, a downspout emptied roof runoff into a wide path adjacent to this garden, so the area was often soggy. The gardener, Peggy Willenberg, added the hose to the drainspout and transformed this garden into an impromptu rain garden. "It was a real do-it-yourself project," she says. When she couldn't find a ready-made solution to distribute the water, she bought a 4-inch diameter flexible drain pipe and drilled the holes in it herself. (Perforated draintile is available from some garden centers; it comes with a sock that should be used in sandy soil to keep the holes from becoming clogged.)

Peggy top-dressed this garden bed with mushroom compost to make it extra absorbent, and she keeps it moist by watering twice a week in dry weather. The hophornbeams are native understory trees that can tolerate this hot, west-facing location if they are given a shady, moist root zone. Their companion plants thrive in moist shade and are protected from the afternoon sun by the overhanging tree foliage.

Many an existing garden could happily absorb redirected roof runoff, especially if the runoff is distributed throughout the garden rather than pouring into one area from the mouth of a drainspout. (Gardens that receive roof runoff should be located at least 10 feet from any wall with a basement.) Shady areas can hold onto moisture longer, and this can exacerbate any problems you may have with pooling and waterlogging. Transforming an existing garden into a rain garden, or making a rain garden in the shade, can be an effective and beautiful solution.

top: The drainage hose at left carries roof runoff through a shady garden, transforming it into a functional rain garden. Virginia bluebells (Mertensia virginica), native large-flowered trillium (T. grandiflorum), and bleeding hearts (Dicentra spectabilis), all seen here in springtime bloom, welcome the extra water.

bottom: Trees not only make a rain garden more effective, they also make it more appealing during every season. Hophornbeams (Ostrya virginiana) form showy hoplike seeds in late July.

patios

Patios add life to a garden by making a place where people can comfortably spend time outdoors. Many people will use a well-designed and -sited patio more often than they would use a lawn. In a tiny yard, when compared to a lawn, a patio gives more usable space, less work, and more potential for vertical features that can add privacy outside and views from within your home.

A patio can be the warm spot in cool weather if it is kept open to the sun. If shaded, and especially if fitted out with plants and a water feature, it can be the cool spot in warm weather. It will dry faster than a lawn after a rain, making it walkable in more types of weather. It can even be shoveled or swept clear of snow in winter, extending your garden's season of use.

Patios add functional space to your home and landscape. They offer a site for heavier furniture that need never be moved or trimmed around. They limit the mud and debris that are tracked into the house. A patio directly outside your door will feel like an extension of your home; you can carry things out onto it—food to be eaten, books to be read, and delicate electronic devices.

The floor of a patio can be a prominent design feature for your garden. Paving patterns may show through all seasons, lending interest when plants are dormant. Planted gaps between pavers and stones add interest too, as they flower or turn color with the seasons.

In a small urban garden, a patio is easily more functional and appealing than a lawn.

You can get creative with the shape as well. A patio doesn't need to be shaped like a circle or square; it can flow around trees, follow the curve of a path, nestle into or wrap around the corner of a building. A stretch of paving can be interrupted and enlivened by a planted island, a pond, or a fire pit. If you build an impervious patio, you can slope it to shed water away from nearby buildings and into an adjacent planting bed.

As with any hardscaping, cost can become an issue. You may be able to save significant money by buying local or using found materials. Though it may take some planning, some work, and some expense, a thoughtfully designed patio can dramatically increase both the extent and quality of your time in the garden.

patio for one

This Saint Paul gardener can't imagine living in a place where she has no garden. When she moved from her home into a condominium, she chose a first-floor unit with its own entrance and negotiated that she be allowed to make a small garden outside her door. She hired workers to enlarge her sidewalk into a patio just large enough for one chair, then she built her garden along both sides of the sidewalk, from her front door to the main walkway. Each bed is roughly 4 feet wide and 15 feet long.

A longtime gardener, she knew that good soil is the key to healthy plants, and with such a small garden she could afford to create her own soil. This was more work at the beginning, but it paid off. Her plants established quickly and are more likely to stay healthy for years to come.

She made a couple of low berms using a rich, light soil mix that she created by blending garden soil, gravel, and processed manure from the garden center. Berming up the garden was a less work-intensive way to add good soil than digging, and as a bonus, it also gave her a bit more gardening surface and more diversity of microclimates, allowing for a wider variety of plants.

Another way to maximize diversity in a small space is to use small plants. She planted many alpines and miniature evergreens on her well-drained berms. Because the plants grow slowly and stay small, her garden won't become a burden to maintain.

This urban garden is tucked into a courtyard enclosed by a raised walkway and two wings of her building. This space also contains a communal patio surrounded with shrubs and trees. She can sit out on her patio and enjoy views of her garden and the larger landscape, and should friends come to visit, the communal patio is readily available.

With a background as a garden center employee advising other gardeners and 28 years of gardening in many

One shrub border shields a semi-private patio and garden from the street, and another softens the view between the garden and a nearby communal patio.

Because of its protected location and the experienced gardener's use of microclimates and careful selection of plants, this northern garden is vibrant and colorful even in October.

places and circumstances, this gardener recognized the value of the sheltering walls, the border of mid-sized shrubs between her garden and the street, and her garden's east-southeast exposure, all of which help to hoard warmth and extend her growing season. Plants come out of dormancy early in spring, are sheltered from late afternoon sun, and are protected from winter winds. She took all this into consideration when choosing and siting plants. Though Saint Paul is considered zone 4 for winter hardiness, she enjoys sprinkling desirable zone 5 plants among the more hardy and dependable perennials. It is a challenge to create a microclimate that might entice one of these less hardy plants to flower. "When

one comes into bloom," she says, "it is a happy day in the garden."

Her garden has attracted admirers since its inception. Neighbors make repeated visits to see how it has changed. Butterflies visit also, finding the milkweed (*Asclepias*) she has planted to offer them nectar and larval food.

In this northern climate, where a layer of snow will likely obscure her own garden all winter, the abundant trees and shrubs in the surrounding landscape provide four-season interest. Red-twig dogwoods (*Cornus sericea*) brighten winter with their showy stems, and dried flowerheads of multiple hydrangea varieties also hold up well through the cold months, catching snow and frost

*A golden fan of variegated purple moor grass (*Molinia caerulea subsp. caerulea *'Variegata') and a flowering, silver-blue mound of lavender (*Lavandula angustifolia *'Munstead') arch their stems above shorter companions.*

for a wintry sculptural display. Early spring brings a burst of white flowers on the serviceberry trees (*Amelanchier ×grandiflora* 'Autumn Brilliance') above the communal patio and emerging red-tinged leaves from the maples. In summer, the hydrangeas and dogwoods bloom together, then the dogwoods produce white berries while the diervillas (*D. lonicera*) bloom yellow. The diervilla foliage, which has an orange cast throughout the growing season, turns red to bronze to brown in the fall. This final splash of color, combined with the brilliant autumn foliage of the serviceberries, dogwoods, and maples, reinforces the

view that this gardener may have the best of both worlds: a small garden packed with many tiny treasures, set in a large, low-care landscape that gives a four-season show.

patio for pennies

Some people are good at creatively using what they have. Whether you don't have the money for landscaping or you would just rather do it yourself, it is entirely possible that materials you find around your property or neighborhood—coupled with imagination and some good old-fashioned elbow grease—are all that you need to create a satisfying home landscape. Your handmade garden may not be a glossy magazine showpiece, but its character will be all your own. You may even cherish it more because you have put more of yourself into it.

The garden shown here was created using very little money. Julie Kostroski, her husband, Jim Polucha, and their two children, Emma and Luke, moved to an old farmhouse in a rural area. Next to the house was a crumbling concrete pad where an old building once stood. Rather than bringing in big machinery to break up and haul away the concrete, then haul in material to fill the holes left by removing it, Julie and Jim repurposed the space themselves to make a comfortable patio.

First they cleared away loose pieces of concrete and debris. Then they filled some of the holes with dirt, sand, and crushed rock they found elsewhere on the property. When they finished, the central area was flat, but it had a lot of cracks, and the edges were uneven where pieces had broken away. They could have lamented their future patio's imperfections; instead they embraced them.

In the largest gaps of this patio-to-be, where roof runoff from the nearby house collected during rainstorms, Julie planted a mix of grasses and flowers, including fireweed (*Chamerion angustifolium*), fox sedge (*Carex vulpinoidea*), oxeye (*Heliopsis helianthoides*), and showy goldenrod (*Solidago speciosa*), to soak up the runoff. Where a large corner of the concrete was broken away, she planted a couple of purple-leaved ninebarks (*Physocarpus opulifolius* 'Center Glow'). Alongside the patio, she created a loose, sheltering wall using plants that are tall and striking, to draw attention from the asymmetric concrete.

Big cracks that ran through the patio were filled with low creepers to keep the floor open and walkable. Low plants include alpine rock cress (*Arabis alpina* subsp. *caucasica*), creeping thyme (*Thymus serpyllum*), and the fragrant, self-sowing sweet alyssum (*Lobularia maritima*). One winter, seven-year-old Emma gathered a "bouquet" of dried flowers and arranged them in the empty patio umbrella stand; the seeds from that bouquet added new plants to the patio cracks.

top: *Cracks in an aged patio were filled with flowers and even a couple of shrubs; this ingenious strategy shows it is possible to be budget- and beauty-conscious at the same time.*

bottom: *Taller plants border the reclaimed patio, bringing attention up and away from the floor.*

The patio overlooks a play area with a sandbox and kiddie pool, and the family uses it often. Many homeowners pay to have a naturalistic patio installed; by paying attention to what was already on their site, this family was able to create such a place with only the cost of a few weeks' labor and some plants and seeds. Though it may not be their "ideal garden," it is a real and pleasurable part of their daily lives.

Being willing to work within your site's constraints and to see them as opportunities often means changing your plan for a place as you get to know it better. That wet spot is never going to be a great rock garden. The compacted, baking boulevard won't support a fern-filled glade. Not without a lot of effort or money, anyway.

Rather than imposing your dream garden on your site, why not adapt your needs and desires to your site's characteristics? If you stop trying to subdue those parts that are quirky or unappealing, you won't have to continually battle the elements and processes present in your garden. You will be freed from your struggle to make the perfect landscape. In a way, it is like giving your garden unconditional love.

hidden gardens

In a densely populated urban area, noises are magnified as they echo against the hard surfaces. Walls of vegetation make a fine visual shield but don't do much to dampen the noise. Fences and walls can block sounds much better, giving you a haven from the bustle of public streets. They can also be the bones of a relaxing urban garden.

As our cities become more populated, open spaces are filled and buildings are set closer together. The spaces left over between buildings are potential oases. Though most of their area may be paved to accommodate walking and seating, with added greenery to soften them and to filter and oxygenate the urban air, these cramped but relatively private spaces can be made to feel cozy.

*A mini-meadow along one side of the patio includes shasta daisies (*Leucanthemum ×superbum*) and prairie sage (*Artemisia ludoviciana*); a purple ninebark (*Physocarpus opulifolius 'Center Glow'*) anchors the corner.*

In the proud city of Pittsburgh, Pennsylvania, lies an unapologetically urban district where front yards practically don't exist, and all you see from the street or sidewalk is asphalt, concrete, bricks, glass, and metal, along with a few trees. But explore further and you will discover that private courtyards abound, giving this part of the city a secret green side. It's an intriguing juxtaposition.

If we cannot see an end to a space, we imagine it might be endless. You can make an enclosed garden feel more spacious by obscuring its sides and corners with

An enclosed entry garden in Pittsburgh soothes the senses with subdued foliage, the trickle of a modest fountain, a cooling stone floor, and a metal door that pays homage to the City of Steel.

Part of the charm of the urban courtyard at Pittsburgh's Morning Glory Inn is the thoughtful inclusion of small-scale sensory details like twinkle lights strung through an arbor and vases of fresh cut flowers.

greenery or other barriers, and by hiding part of the garden from view with eye-level foliage or screening. Other techniques for making a small space larger include varying your path materials and adding tall plants and vertical structures. These increase the surface area of the garden. Also, cool pastel tones such as light blue, pink, and lavender tend to recede from our view, making them seem more distant, while warm yellows and reds pull us toward them. Using cool colors in your small garden will make it feel larger, and combining close-up warm colors with far-away cool colors also works well. "Borrowing" a distant view by framing it with foliage can make your garden feel larger too.

What a haven an enclosed garden provides! The relative darkness and quiet invite you to open your senses, and the sheltering walls concentrate the aromatic oils of the plants. Sink into a chair in a leafy corner. As a relaxed setting for socializing or solitude in an urban area, nothing beats a hidden oasis.

Magnify the sensory delights of your next meal.

living more outdoors

Think how much more of nature you'll see if you spend more time outdoors—eating a meal, drinking wine with your friends, or reading the paper—where the cicadas will serenade you, and where you will notice that newly opened flower that was only a bud yesterday. Imagine training grapevines to grow on the arbor above your patio, then picking the fresh fruit and eating it while reclining on your deckchair. Imagine never having to move that deckchair to mow under it. Imagine how peaceful it will feel if you never mow again.

To tune out other noises, like your neighbor's motorcycle or the dog across the alley, try a wind chime or fountain. A small trickle of water falling into a basin or half-barrel can take up very little space, be affordable, and give you hours of priceless peace. If you also plant some berry-bearing shrubs, the chirping of your new avian friends might just drown out the sound of your phone ringing unanswered as you relax in your restorative natural retreat.

For visual privacy and more four-season interest, as well as a better view of your patio garden from inside the house, add trellises, a fence, or a hedge around part or all of your patio. If you are in a climate with cold winters, well-placed vertical structures can block cold winds and extend the season for using your patio. If you experience hot, humid summers, you may want to keep a "breeze-way" open to let cooling air flow through but add a roof over the patio for welcome shade.

A patio can make your quality of life soar by bringing nature further into your life. If you don't mow, you can significantly increase your animal population. Capitalize on this and welcome more wildlife by choosing other less intrusive maintenance strategies too—for instance, sweeping instead of strapping on the leaf blower.

We humans are social creatures, and regular doses of time spent among our loved ones will make our lives more meaningful and more satisfying. So if your life is a busy one, all the more reason to take time for appreciating those connections. You have to eat…why not eat with friends? Why not do it outside where you can look up at the sky, and feel the breeze, and laugh at the antics of a resident chipmunk?

on the surface

Maintenance-wise, a hard surface in general needs much less attention than a lawn. It doesn't demand regular mowing or watering, and you don't have to move the furniture (except maybe to sweep leaves away in autumn). Keeping weeds out will likely be the only regular concern.

The exception is loose gravel: unless it is very deep, it could easily be more work than a lawn. Shallow gravel holds enough moisture at the soil surface to create an ideal seedbed for many plants. In fact, it may significantly increase germination of seedlings from nearby plants. To prevent it from harboring prolific seedlings, rake it daily or at least every few days with a short-tined metal rake. This will also move particles of dust and debris below the surface, keeping it fresh and well textured.

Impervious surfaces like poured concrete and mortared pavers, rocks, or bricks will need the least regular care. Periodically they can be swept to keep debris from collecting in any hollows and inviting volunteer plants to germinate. Every few years or so, the mortar may need to be renewed. Packed gravel can also be kept looking well with periodic sweeping and a fresh layer every few years.

The biggest potential issue for impervious surfaces is the runoff they will generate if located in a less-than-permeable landscape. This can be addressed in your design. To help your patio quickly and effectively shed water, slightly slope it to direct runoff into a planting bed or other absorbent landscape. This is especially important if

Herbs all around, including rosemary in the foreground, make a deliciously scented seating area.

your patio is located next to a building, and is a good idea for permeable patios too.

A paved patio with unmortared gaps can also absorb some runoff depending on the base materials used. In climates with little rain, a 2-inch base of sand or gravel may be enough to keep the pavement dry. Use a deeper gravel base in wetter climates so the runoff can flow out under the paving stones.

Gaps between pavers can increase the regular maintenance that your patio needs to look its best. Plants can find their ways into the cracks in any type of environment: sunny or shady, dry or damp, acidic or alkaline. You may be able to keep the gaps in your patio free of plants with regular sweeping, some weeding, occasional power-washing, or chemical weedkillers, but all these methods cost effort or money, and the last two are downright unfriendly to wildlife. A friendlier approach that will also mean less work for you in the long run is to either plant the gaps or selectively edit the "volunteers" that arrive.

Gaps that are filled by your chosen plants will resist weeds and even tree seedlings. With only occasional weeding from you and perhaps a trim every few years, these plants will keep your patio relatively weed-free. They will also help it to infiltrate more runoff, as each plant's roots will permeate a patch of soil and create an absorbent pocket in the patio.

Idaho gardener Doug Becker designed a low-mainte-nance rock patio with woolly thyme (*Thymus pseudola-nuginosus*) planted in the gaps between slabs of locally quarried quartzite. The rocks are laid on a foundation of sand, so the patio is very well drained. The thyme grows easily in the sand-filled gaps and spreads out across the sun-baked surfaces of the rocks. Doug paid good money for the rocks and enjoys looking at them, so every few years he trims back the thyme that threatens to obscure them. It takes about 15 minutes and requires only a bag, a pair of clippers, gloves, and a rake.

"It's just like trimming a comb-over," he says with a grin. First he rakes back the loose thyme that has sprawled over the rocks. Then he clips the loose portions off, rakes them up, and bags them. The bag of clippings makes a great gift for a gardening friend; the clippings will root easily if scattered across bare, sandy soil and kept watered.

Doug doesn't necessarily think that the woolly thyme makes his rock patio look better, but he appreciates the functions it performs and the work it saves him. He prefers not to use chemicals in maintaining his yard, as he lives next to a lake and realizes pesticides and fertil-izers can wash into the water and have a negative effect on aquatic life. He has partnered with nature, opting for a landscape design that minimizes his workload and is healthy for the larger landscape.

Woolly thyme is just one of many plants that can be used to fill gaps in and among pavers. Almost any mat-former will work, and a plant with a fragrance, like chocolate mint (*Mentha ×piperita* f. *citrata* 'Chocolate') or Roman chamomile (*Chamaemelum nobile*), can make walk-ing across your patio a more sensual experience.

Creatively mixing the hard materials of your patio will enhance its allure and year-round interest, especially in climates where the patio will not be buried in snow but can be enjoyed during winter too. Simple borders or stripes add flair, and an artistic inlaid design can carry the visual power of a large sculpture.

top: Doug Becker spends about 15 minutes every three years to maintain his rock-and-thyme patio.

bottom: D.C. gardener Barbara Dinsmore never tires of the beauty of the "stream" that runs through her patio. "What a calming, natural, and clever idea for such a small garden as this."

play areas

Young children need to move, and most parents look for a way to provide a home outdoor environment where their kids can run and play with supervision until they are old enough to roam further afield. Lawns give kids a soft, safe place to run and play in plain sight, which is important for their physical development; however, lawns alone cannot provide the outdoor experiences that growing kids need. Nor can playsets or other built structures, say researchers.

Brain development requires stimulation, and research shows that the greater scope and variety of sensory encounters a child has, the more complex that child's brain structure will be. The documented, measurable benefits for children who spend time in natural settings include higher self-esteem, improved ability to concentrate, more creative and cooperative play, and increased self-direction. To develop their brains as well as their motor skills and other physical abilities, kids want and need to be exploring, hiding, climbing, imagining, and dreaming, using their different senses to learn about the world, engaging in creative and social play, and interacting with other species. A more natural outdoor environment is a perfect place to support all these aspects of a child's development. Natural places are filled with sound, scent, textures, color, and movement, making them excellent environments for growing bodies and minds.

Though not a suitable play area for unsupervised toddlers, a sophisticated perennial garden amplifies the appeal of the small lawn and standard playset. As Lucy Maud Montgomery's Anne of Green Gables might say, it provides "scope for the imagination."

Nature centers and botanical gardens are leading the way in incorporating natural elements to make more stimulating, more fulfilling play areas for kids. Parents can get ideas for adding new dimensions of experience to their own yards by visiting public children's gardens. The main message from the experts is this: make a wilder outdoor play area, and let your child be wilder outdoors.

running, hiding, climbing

Interactive adventure gardens engage children's minds and bodies by providing a variety of environments and encouraging many different activities. They are interesting enough to drown out the siren call of video games and television, at least temporarily. They also help children to develop their own sense of safety and territory; kids move more confidently through space as they collect experiences in which they are apart from adults (even if they are supervised from a distance). Children derive an unshakable sense of belonging from making or finding their own special outdoor places, where they can interact with natural elements including soil, water, plants, and animals.

Anyone familiar with kids knows that they must run. An open expanse of lawn can be handy for a ball game, but a wide path that makes a loop around a planted island will create more excitement as vistas appear and disappear around each bend. This "peek-a-boo" experience allows kids to repeatedly sample the fear of being out of your sight and strengthens their self-confidence and self-reliance within a safe setting.

What could you plant in that island bed? A grove of sumacs, bamboo, bananas, or another suckering tall plant that will create hiding places and allow children to squirm between or make trails through a maze of closely set trunks. Kids love exploring child-sized spaces like the little low-ceilinged caves created by arching branches. Inside a shrub, you are surrounded by the fragrance and colors and sounds of the foliage, pressed up against the bark, privy to the secrets hidden in the dense center: a mossy chickadee nest, or a bright cluster of berries, or a handsome beetle. Add a zesty groundcover of shade-tolerant, traffic-resistant, edible spearmint.

Surprise motivates continued exploration. Children are especially geared to seek out the new as part of their work of making sense of the world. Ducking through an arch or tunnel, going around a corner, peering through a veil of greenery or a peephole cut into a fence, all give a sense of adventure and heighten the excitement of being in the garden. A winding path with things to see and do along it, or a labyrinth made with tall annual zinnias or cosmos, can also make an enticing game of exploration.

For a quicker structure, train vines like scarlet runner bean (*Phaseolus coccineus*) with its tender, edible pods, or firecracker vine (*Ipomoea lobata*), whose flowers make a loud pop when squeezed, up a teepee made from trimmed tree branches roped together at the top. Or plant a sunflower house. Or drag an old table out into the garden and plant celosias, amaranths, and other colorful and texturally engaging annuals around it. Playhouses offer a more durable shelter. They can house toys and "found treasures" between games, and they provide a dry place for a tea party during a rainstorm.

The goal of climbing is to look down and survey the territory, and to marvel at one's own agility and bravery. It also develops coordination and limberness in differ-ent muscles than running does. For these reasons and more, kids appreciate the opportunity to climb. This is the job of the traditional playset, but other possible and less costly climbing places include towers, trees with low branches or prominent burls, safely stacked rocks, leaning logs, and rope ladders. Even better than climb-ing is climbing up to some secret lookout. It could be a treehouse, or a simple raised platform partly concealed by tall shrubs. It could even be a path or staircase up a hill to a hidden clearing at the top.

top: Protected by fences and hedges, a looping path around a mysteri-ous vine-covered arbor is perfectly designed for a safe adventure.

bottom: A well-loved play-house sits at the corner of a yard, next to a garden of bite-size cherry tomatoes and other child-friendly plants.

above: Structures that serve other purposes can be made sturdy enough for climbing.

left: A stick and a body of water add up to hours of enjoyable play.

For the ultimate in interactive adventure gardens, give children a place they can run in a circle around, hide in, and climb up into when they are being chased.

child-friendly water features

For children (and for many adults as well), one of the most essential and intriguing natural elements in a garden is water. Sensual, interactive, and ever-changing, water draws children like a magnet, and they will stay and play for hours. Even a small mud puddle holds astonishing allure; it can be poked at with a stick, and splashed, and the mud used for war paint or trail markings.

There are many ways to build water into a garden so that children can safely incorporate it into their play. A shallow pond, even a temporary one in a plastic kiddie pool, encourages wading and can mellow the crankiest mood on a hot day. Moving water increases the potential for interaction, and the excitement. A shallow stream running through a garden brings opportunities for fishing, racing sticks, building dams, and floating small boats. If you have the means, a shallow waterfall makes a magical play place. A safe alternative for toddlers is a bubbler or fountain that emerges from the ground and can be stood in, waded through, even sat upon. Or make your own fountain in a shallow bowl, and supply it with stones that can be moved around to change the sound and flow.

If you do plan to invest in some landscaping, why not incorporate a water feature that can be used for play and will also beautify your garden? A swimming hole that looks like a lagoon, with a graveled or sandy beach, can put your backyard on par with any vacation destination. How much more appealing daily life becomes when you are living at the lake instead of just wishing you were there! Even the most memorable vacation can't compete with a home landscape that lets your family experience the wonders of nature every day.

creativity boosters

One way to stimulate young imaginations is to include prompts or props that will suggest stories and fantasies they can act out in the garden. Themes based on real or fictional characters familiar to children will engage them and speed their connection to a place. Bringing their toys into a landscape can help kids to interact more closely with the unfamiliar using the familiar as a bridge. They will often act out their fears and anxieties on these toys, sending them into danger and then rescuing them. This type of play helps kids to face the unknown with less anxiety and more confidence in their ability to handle unexpected threats.

However, research on creative play suggests that the best objects for strengthening a child's creativity are those that can be used in many different situations and

Gauzy "scarves" dangle from a jungle gym at Lewis Ginter Botanical Garden, Richmond, Virginia.

imagined to be many things. "Everything that's around us is a potential prop for creative play," says Randee Humphrey, director of education at Lewis Ginter Botanical Garden in Richmond, Virginia. This public garden includes a large multi-faceted Children's Garden with, among other props, a bottomless basket of bright, gauzy squares. These "scarves" have been used for games in every part of the garden, inspiring dances and dress-up play. "It doesn't take a whole lot to suddenly make something seem magical," says Randee. Part of her mission—a mission shared by public children's gardens across the country—is to come up with easy, inexpensive ideas that parents can try at home to give their kids more fulfilling outdoor play experiences.

According to the NatureGrounds program, a cooperative effort between playset designers and child development researchers to create safe and stimulating play areas,

Rocks and other natural materials inspire creative play. Kids create their own rock sculptures at Hershey Children's Garden in Cleveland.

child-friendly plants include those that "produce loose parts that inspire creative and socio-dramatic play." Yes, the very plants that we disparage as "messy" are quite stimulating to a child, because their loose parts can be used as props. The long pods of catalpa trees, the fluff inside cattails, birch catkins, and maple whirlybirds all make strong sensory memories and grist for the imagination.

The variability in textures, colors, and shapes of natural materials also promotes interest and sensory exploration. A box of pine cones or a pile of acorns can be used in all kinds of imaginative endeavors. Think of the many ways that kids interact with autumn leaves, from making rubbings, to lying on the ground and looking up as they fall, to raking up a pile and jumping in them. Sand boxes are a classic example of a natural material providing hours of easy and inexpensive fun. Play is especially satisfying when it involves the entire body, like running does, and swimming, and rolling down hills, and simply sitting in sand and moving it from place to place.

companionable plants and animals

Elements that move are infinitely appealing to children. Waving grasses, fluttering leaves, and any live creature will engage them. Interacting with the world, especially the plants and animals in it, intensifies their interest and awareness, and it can create heightened memories that will stir them to make future connections with natural places and with other species.

Many kids love to meet plants that are edible. Give them a string bean or raspberry patch, and they may become fascinated with growing food plants, or learning more about plants in general. Try herbs too; most kids love mint but will also try a surprising number of other herbs, just for the fun and newness of eating a leaf right out of the garden. Some to try include anise hyssop (*Agastache foeniculum*) for its black licorice flavor, tangy lemon balm (*Melissa officinalis*), the sweet seeds and leaves

Six-year-old Levi, bug lover and avid collector, displays a sphinx moth that he raised from a goliath hornworm. His supportive family gladly sacrificed a couple of their tomato plants, which are the moth's larval food, in the process.

A lawn holds little interest for Clara when there are chives to be harvested.

Plants can be incorporated into play (or snacked on), with a child's kitchen handily located next to the herb garden.

of fennel (*Foeniculum vulgare*), mild dill (*Anethum graveolens*) for contrast, and even spicy basil (*Ocimum basilicum*). Lamb's ear (*Stachys byzantina*) is also edible, and this can be fun as it is so furry. There are many more to sample.

Cultivate your and your children's sense of wonder by seeking out and growing unusual plants—really big plants, really small plants, plants with odd seedheads or flowers, and other wonders of nature. Some of the plant parts can become the raw materials for projects (like gourd birdhouses, lavender sachets, catnip-stuffed cat toys, sage wreaths, cut flowers and branches) to decorate the house or give as gifts.

To help your kids grow to love and appreciate the special qualities of plants, make it easy for them to incorporate plants into their play by including child-friendly plants near play areas. Plants that can be touched and are enjoyable to touch will be viewed as friends and playmates, earning a place in games, accompanying children into their "dens," and being focused on with all the senses.

Many plants can provide soft spots for kids to sit, lie, or walk on. A diversity of these planted surfaces will allow children to experience different textures with their hands, feet, and bodies. A springy low sedum makes a surprisingly enjoyable "bed" and gives your feet a gentle massage when walked across. Soft woolly thyme, chamomile, and yarrow give off aromas when crushed underfoot.

Scents are powerful memory anchors. Many of us can recall special fragrances associated with our childhood. Shade-loving violets make a flowery and delicately perfumed carpet inside a sunflower house or a twig tunnel.

Hedges and thickets with aromatic leaves (spicebush, *Lindera benzoin*) or fragrant flowers (mock orange, *Philadelphus lewisii*) can allow total immersion in the scented air. Including aromatic plants in your garden will give your kids a lifetime of rich sensory memories, and a group of plants that will be familiar friends if not beloved companions throughout their lives.

In days past, climbing trees played a significant role in many a childhood. More than just a play structure or hiding place, a familiar large tree becomes a confidant, a comforter, perhaps even a confessor, or (when used as a perch to lob things at unsuspecting victims) a comrade in arms.

A mulberry tree (*Morus rubra*) in the center of the Children's Garden at Lewis Ginter Botanical Garden is a local legend with a venerable history and strong personality. There are defining moments in a child's life, and climbing this tree, with its enormous contorted limbs curving along the ground and up into the air, is guaranteed to be one of them. Not just because of its awesome stature, and not even because climbing it (with care) is encouraged, but because when they have climbed it and are sitting on a high limb, they will feel different. Perched—or held—in this tree's canopy, they become a part of a larger wildness. And they feel wilder too.

Even if you are past the age where you want to be climbing trees, watching your child—or any child—as they savor that freedom and exhilaration can allow you to recapture your own wildness. You can exercise your own imagination and revel along with that child in this essential part of our inner nature.

The well-loved mulberry tree growing in the Children's Garden at Lewis Ginter Botanical Garden, Richmond, has hosted entire classes of children in its branches.

ponds

A reflecting pool adds ever-changing light and movement to its surroundings.

a pond can outperform a lawn as a low, open expanse to look across from your home or patio, bringing light, movement, wildlife, and possibilities for play into your garden. If not completely covered by plants, the water's surface will reflect ambient light into the surrounding landscape and even into your house. During the day, watery "waves" may move across your walls, and on moonlit nights, your patio or maybe even your bedroom can be bathed in soft light.

In contrast to the very limited biological activity in, around, and under your lawn, ponds teem with abundant and diverse life. They provide waystations for birds and other creatures who are passing through; everyone appreciates a periodic drink and perhaps a bath. They develop populations of frogs, turtles, dragonflies, and other animals who need to live near water. They make it more likely that terrestrial birds and mammals will nest nearby and raise their young within an easy hop or swoop of the water. When your view includes a pond, there is simply much more to see.

There can be more to do as well. Ponds make great play areas, for adults as well as children. Remember the old swimming hole? Tie a rope to an overhead tree branch, and you guarantee days of summer fun for your kids and their friends. If you don't have a natural pond that is swimmable, find a swimming pool designer who specializes in creating naturalistic lagoons and other pond/pool hybrids. If you worry about dosing your play area with chemicals to keep the water clean, look for a designer who can incorporate innovative biofiltration methods, like sending your pool water through an adjacent wetland garden for cleansing. This can make your pond both safer and prettier.

Don't forget to include in your design some exciting features to enable a variety of experiences. A beach invites barefoot walks and wading. A bridge or stepping stones can bring you out into the water. Islands and peninsulas provide more planting space and make more nooks and crannies to shelter nesting birds, sipping foxes, or crouching children.

backyard getaway

Lisa Weidema, Gerald "Bert" Bertelsen, and Lisa's mom, Ora Mae, share a house in a Minneapolis suburb. Their fenced backyard is sunny, about 70 feet square, with a few mature trees at the property line. About seven years ago, Lisa and Bert dug a small oval in the center of the existing lawn, added a pond liner and a pump with a bubbling fountain, and encircled the new pond with rocks for stability. They made the pond 4 feet deep to ensure it wouldn't freeze solid during the winter, meaning they could keep fish in it year-round instead of overwintering them in containers in the garage, as many cold-climate pond owners do. They added a few koi—the prettycolored Japanese carp. Each fish was named, and it was a tragic day when a visiting blue heron snatched up several of them; however, the remaining fish settled in happily

A naturalistic pond, landscaped with drifts of plants (many native), graces the California home of Peter and Sue LaTourrette. The garden took eight months to complete, but it has saved many hours of lawn work and brought many hours of pleasure. "I think a lawn is really boring after the kids grow up and don't need it for play," says Peter.

A habitat pond enlivens a xeric garden.

and had babies within a couple of years. The entire household agreed their new watery ecosystem was much more interesting than the lawn, so they decided to add more habitat for their larger fish population.

With the help of a local landscape designer, they updated their pond…and it now covers the entire backyard. It includes a looping stream, a small waterfall, a gravel beach, and an island accessible by a wooden bridge.

This new landscape has transformed their lives. Mornings include fish-feeding and coffee on the deck overlooking the pond, and Ora Mae does her crossword in a pondside patio chair. Lisa has developed a keen interest in constructing other water features; she has built several small bubblers and fountains and is working on a miniature stream. She has also learned a lot about plants as she continues to add trees, shrubs, mosses, and other woodland groundcovers to the landscape each year. Last but

not least, she has become an amateur photographer, using her camera to explore her increasingly diverse backyard landscape.

The maintenance for this rewarding landscape is remarkably low. Mowing and watering are a distant memory. There are no filters to clean; water is pumped to the top of the stream and is naturally filtered as it moves through 7 feet of rock. Together with the pond plants, this keeps the water clear. The only real work is using a net to remove leaves from the pond, and Lisa says this happens when she feels like doing it. In the winter, she shuts off the pump, disconnects the tube above it, and opens up the check valve. She keeps a couple of smaller pumps running all winter to aerate the pond for the fish. Given the choice between a pond and a lawn, she says, "I would take a pond any day! Once the pond is established in its ecosystem, it is so easy."

bird watchers' pond

Landscape designers Lee Zieke and Lindsay Lee of Willowglen Nursery in Decorah, Iowa, spend most mornings in their screened porch, enjoying the avian activity in their 15-year-old garden. They have set up several birdfeeders and left some snags (standing dead trees) to entice the woodpeckers, and their graveled driveway is perfect for dustbaths. But the centerpiece of the garden, for the birds as well as the people, is their pond.

Stretching along the back side of their house just off the screened porch and the back patio, their pond is technically a wide stream, with a low waterfall near one end and a stone plank bridge across the center. Both ends are obscured by dense woody areas. Several large silver-leaved Siberian bugloss (*Brunnera macrophylla* 'Jack Frost') and other low plants preserve the view of open water from the house. Taller plants rise up along the opposite shore. A two-toned jewelweed (*Impatiens balfourii*) is allowed to self-sow "with supervision" throughout the garden, as it

top left: Most summer evenings (and even some winter ones) are spent "on the island," around a crackling fire.

bottom left: The fish overwinter in the unfrozen depths of their original pond, but in warmer weather they venture into the shallows and swim freely across the entire backyard.

top right: The stream flows around the island even in winter, naturally filtering the water through rock as it circulates and providing a year-round ecosystem for the fish.

bottom right: A fence of willow hoops often supports a line of birds who are waiting their turn to bathe in the shallow falls.

attracts hummingbirds and blooms into the early fall; this plant can be invasive in moist shady areas, but Lindsay says it hasn't wandered out of the pond area.

The pond catches light and sends shimmering reflections up against the overhanging tree foliage. It also brings life and nature right to their back door. Lindsay and Lee, both experienced and enthusiastic bird watchers, have spotted a diverse list of migrating birds as well as nesting pairs in their garden. The land surrounding their house is a natural woodland with a stream, but by making their immediate garden wildlife-friendly, they have been able to entice birds closer so they can more easily observe and enjoy them.

Along the shoreline, dense clusters of primrose (Primula japonica) make dark, moist shelters for bug-eating amphibians and spiders.

On the back patio, between the house and the pond, birds find ants and seeds in crevices, and creeping, slithering, and hopping creatures can take cover under various seedlings as they travel through the sedum-filled joints between the stones. A corner is filled with the delicate foliage of dwarf goatsbeard (*Aruncus aethusifolius*), offering shelter for prey animals who would rather not brave the open expanse of pavement. From a purely aesthetic point of view, the patio is a rich blend of textures and forms, offering a lot of small-scale scenery.

Including sheltered zones, however small, and keeping the cracks unmortared lets more tiny animals move across any paved area. It provides safety from predators and protection from the sun for amphibians and others who need it. These creatures can be entertaining and enjoyable to watch, and they can also make an area more comfortable. Toads are pest predators, eating mosquitoes, flies, and many of the other insects and slugs that damage garden plants. Frogs are welcome pond inhabitants, for their pleasing voices and also because they eat mosquito larvae.

Frog's-eye view of the patio, with its wildlife-friendly mops of vernal sedge (Carex 'The Beatles') and columbine (Aquilegia) seedlings dotted about like toad arbors.

A hardscape devoid of small shelters can cut your landscape into habitable islands that are separated from each other by uncrossable areas. This reduces populations of all species by cutting off access to potential mates and limiting their range and thus their food supply. And the fewer

ants and small crawly creatures, the less "baby food" your landscape holds to entice nesting birds. But if you follow Lee and Lindsay's example, making your pavement crossable from a small creature's point of view, you will be treated to more views of small creatures.

urban revival

When Roy and Rosadelia Detwiler retired, they decided to stay in their longtime home in the San Francisco Bay area but to reinvent their landscape. They enlisted the help of landscape designer Kelly Marshall, of Kelly Marshall Garden Design, who focuses on creating environmentally friendly landscapes that need less care to remain beautiful. Their struggling back lawn was not missed, replaced with a patchwork of water and hardscape that offers plenty of places to cook, eat, and relax outside.

A trio of self-cleaning ponds circulates water through connecting channels that run between large paving stones, making less work for the Detwilers and eliminating the need for chemicals and filters. A main pond with a waterfall pumps the water to a bog, which uses aquatic plants and gravel to filter the water before sending it to a lily pond; from the lily pond, it is pumped back to the main pond. This continual biofiltration keeps the pond water clean and clear.

The garden is landscaped with drought-tolerant plants that attract butterflies. Nectar plants are included for the adults, as well as larval food plants to host the cocoon and caterpillar stages. Most of the plants are native to the region and could survive without extra water; however, they are given some supplemental water to keep them looking their best through the dry season, which typically lasts five months. Watering is done infrequently but deeply using drip irrigation, a strategy that Roy says cut their household water bill by about a third.

Maintaining their paradise takes minimal effort: going through a couple of times per year with the clippers to cut down plants that are past their prime, with some light pruning and deadheading during the growing season. In return, they get a comfortable outdoor setting enlivened by plants and animals, in which they can relax and enjoy nature's beauty. Since they converted their back lawn to this more nature-friendly landscape, they have been privileged to have hummingbirds nest above their outdoor dining table. Pacific chorus frogs have arrived to hatch from clouds of eggs on the surface of the lily pond. Quail have laid eggs under shrubs and raised their brood in the garden. After a couple of years, Roy and Rosadelia took their lawn conversion into their front yard, and now their meals, many of which are cooked and eaten outdoors, include freshly picked food from an edible garden.

The Detwilers welcome the liveliness of their new landscape, but Roy admits his favorite thing about not having a lawn is not having a lawn mower. "I don't even miss it!"

top left: This urban backyard has become a watery habitat enjoyed by hummingbirds, frogs, butterflies, quail, and carefree retirees.

bottom left: Native plants in this pondscape include feathery mounds of Cape Mendocino reed grass (Calamagrostis foliosa) along the path, and a tall stand of showy milkweed (Asclepias speciosa), a butterfly larval food, at right.

top right: Another native, California gray rush (Juncus patens), is featured in the bog.

bottom right: Their revived landscape makes cooking and eating a wild experience.

xeric gardens

A comfortable xeric land-
scape combines warm-hued
walls and paving with wildly
blooming, waterwise gaura
(G. lindheimeri).

all arid landscapes—from low grasslands to mountain timberline, from scattered shrublands to deserts dotted with cacti—share common visual traits that set them apart from wetter landscapes. You'll see plenty of silver foliage, and bare ground between the plants. Whole seasons pass, painted in golds and browns. Distant views of mountains or sky are an ever-present reminder of the vastness of nature. But even in a desert, it is possible to make an abundant and colorful garden with well-chosen plants that need much less water than a typical turfgrass lawn. As a gardener living in an arid climate, you can capitalize on the inherent drama of succulents, the starkness of shadows, the welcome coolness of evenings, and the bright colors that show well in sunlight unclouded by moisture.

Xeric gardens need not be barren. You don't have to give up your roses or even your tomatoes. Smart watering techniques like drip irrigation and moisture-sensing controllers make efficient use of a precious resource. You can enlist rainwater to passively irrigate your plants and decrease their dependence on you. You can subtly shape the earth so that the little precipitation you do get is channeled to your plants instead of evaporating or flowing away off your property.

*Hand-sculpted adobe paving stones interlaced with woolly thyme (*Thymus pseudolanuginosus*), a courtyard encircled by a stuccoed strawbale wall, and a built-in bread and pizza oven celebrate outdoor living in a dry climate. Native desert four o'clock (*Mirabilis multiflora*) blooms at right.*

Many plants with colorful flowers and dramatic forms have evolved to live in dry places. Landscaping with these dry-adapted plants can decrease your workload and make your garden more texturally interesting, in addition to providing bold-colored blooms that bring in the hummingbirds. Because the plants tend to accent rather than dominate the landscape, you have an opportunity to make a bigger impact with your hardscape and other non-plant materials, including sculptures, significant rock features, patterned paving, and painted walls.

A garden that uses elements suited to your region—local rock, native or other dry-adapted plants—will not only take less care and less cost to maintain, it can offer crucial habitat to local and visiting wildlife. It can bring your region's nature to your doorstep so you can enjoy it daily: the intensity of sunlight, the vast sky, the wobbling

gait of quail or sleek streak of roadrunners, the dusty perfume of sagebrush. It can celebrate what is unique and special about your location and make those qualities a part of your home landscape and your daily life.

dry drama

Garden writer and landscape architect Billy Goodnick collaborated with artistic homeowners to create a memorable Southern California hillside garden on a 40- by 60-foot west-facing slope. The homeowners were interested in a bold look; Billy suggested four big masses of plantings, like jigsaw puzzle pieces, then selected strongly contrasting combinations of foliage color and textures for each piece. "The big idea," says Billy, "was that guests would have no problem picking out their house."

Not only does the new garden give visitors a colorful welcome, it has also transformed the view from inside the house; the olive trees do a great job of screening out the residential street while preserving the long view of mountains and sunsets. The thick cover of the plants and their running (*Tradescantia*) and deep (*Nassella*) root structures hold the soil against erosion. When it does rain, instead of washing down the slope to the pavement below, precious water is slowed and absorbed into the soil. And though the homeowners still irrigate, they now use a drip system, which delivers water directly to the plant roots with minimal evaporation and runoff.

For the first few years of its life, this hillside garden needed vigilant hand-weeding while the new plants took hold and filled in their territories. Now the main "weeding" involves occasionally keeping the groundcovers within bounds to preserve the puzzle piece pattern. Other maintenance includes structural pruning to help shape the trees, deadheading the kangaroo paw, and shearing the feather grass to the ground each late winter.

Converting this unloved lawn (Billy describes its "before" look as a "big eyesore of bermudagrass and weeds,

scorched in the summer, too steep to water and mow") to a dramatic, dry-adapted garden is part of Billy's larger mission to "demystify landscape design for average folks so they can create beautiful, useful, sustainable gardens." A founding member of the Lawn Reform Coalition, he's particularly hard on water-hogging lawns grown in low-rain areas. "In dry climates, the only acceptable reason for a residential lawn is if it gets used for recreation," he says. "If a lawn is the only logical choice for a garden floor, it should be the smallest possible size and be cared for with respect for resources and harmful impacts."

left: Bold stripes of ground-layer plants make this small streetside slope a traffic stopper. Under a young olive tree (Olea europaea), purple heart (Tradescantia pallida) is backed by glow-ing Mexican feather grass (Nassella tenuissima).

right: In this jigsaw piece, century plant (Agave attenuata) is paired with purple heart (Tradescantia pallida). Kangaroo paw (Anigozanthos) blooms in the background by the front door.

Recurring groundcovers—
bright orange California
poppy (Eschscholzia califor-
nica), yellow sulphur flower
(Eriogonum umbellatum),
and a low, white-flowering
sedum—bring continuity to
this diverse xeric garden.

As autumn approaches, color
comes from long-blooming
perennials like blanketflower
(Gaillardia), orange-toned
dry flowerheads of sulphur
flower (Eriogonum umbel-
latum), and the yellow fall
blooms of sage (Artemisia)
and gray rabbitbrush
(Ericameria nauseosa).

lusher than lawn

This 12-year-old xeric garden, one of the oldest in Boise, Idaho, is located on a main road near downtown. The small front yard and boulevard overflow with a many-textured community of drought-tolerant flowering plants, and native high desert shrubs echo those in the surrounding scrub-clad foothills. This garden shows how you can combine well-adapted plants in a way that is beautiful to the eye but still reflects the character of a region.

Shrubs near the front windows completely screen the busy street from view. Locating taller plants in the centers of the main beds makes a pleasing many-layered view from the street and sidewalk, with lower plants flowing among the taller ones and occasionally spilling out onto the pavement. This gives a strong impression of abundance that is unusual and welcome in an arid setting, and that is entirely possible in a desert garden with smart siting, good preparation, and waterwise irrigation. As these plants are spaced more closely than they would be in nature, they need supplemental water to thrive and bloom. A drip irrigation system directs water to their roots with minimal evaporation; evaporation is a primary water user in arid regions, and the sooner the water can be absorbed in the soil, the more water you save.

This dry-climate garden offers a glimpse of the future. When drinking water becomes (or where it is already) too scarce or too expensive to spend on desert lawns, then well-designed gardens can bring new life to arid landscapes. Partnering our human ingenuity with nature, we can design and build gardens that require much less water and labor to flourish. We can rely on natural processes like the relentless flow of water, the insulating properties of rock, and the water-conserving strategies of dry-adapted plants to sustain these gardens with minimal help and resources from the gardener. In addition, these landscapes can be true oases, providing shelter and food to desert wildlife and migrating butterflies and birds.

bold and bright

Dry-adapted plants do not resemble the massive trees and large-leaved understory plants of wetter woodlands. They are parsimonious with their plant material. They hoard moisture and use it efficiently, creating structures that help them withstand sun and drought—smaller leaves with waxy covers to retain more water and take in less sun, or thick rubbery storage chambers that save up water, with spines to deter animal thieves. Plants may grow up in long columns, exposing the least surface area to the desiccating sun, rather than sprawling across the ground in water-wasting profusion.

*White-flowered jupiter's beard (*Centranthus ruber *'Albus') provides a night light when the sun sinks low on this desert patio.*

As a result, xeric landscapes can feel downright friendly; the plants aren't generally overwhelming in size and they are spaced apart, allowing plenty of visibility. There is room to move between and among them. Such an open, inviting landscape prompts people to leisurely explore. You may find yourself wandering here and there to peer at some colorful bloom or striking form that has attracted your interest from afar.

Dry-adapted plants offer an opportunity to create dramatically painted landscapes. Many penstemons, salvias, red hot pokers (*Kniphofia*), montbretias (*Crocosmia*), and other bright-blooming plants native to dry areas, and even low-growing plants like opuntias, have long-lasting flowers that make a big visual splash even from a distance, and they will often attract hummingbirds, bees, and butterflies. These colors can create a lighter, livelier mood when not counterbalanced by green surroundings. Silvery foliage is also common in arid regions as it reflects the sun's rays and can keep a plant cooler; it reflects moonlight too, giving the garden a ghostly glow in the evenings and early mornings.

A commonly occurring plant shape in dry landscapes is the spiky mound. These plants have stark lines that draw attention, and they can be used to create patterns or rhythms in the landscape. For a simple but dramatic pairing, underplant spiky mounding plants—adam's needle (*Yucca*), century plant (*Agave*), red yucca (*Hesperaloe*), kangaroo paw (*Anigozanthos*), New Zealand flax (*Phormium*)—with low, creeping groundcovers.

Arid regions undergo dramatic seasonal changes. Their colors shift from a brief, lush green in the wet spring to a colorful flush of bloom in early summer, then they slowly turn to brown, gold, bronze, gray, blue, and even pink as the summer progresses, with a blaze of reds and golds in fall. A garden that follows this lyrical color progression is more interesting than a one-note lawn. Grasses in particular will provide this changeable quality, and even the lower species, when massed, can be a bold and dynamic

element in the garden. Blue-green sheep fescue (*Festuca ovina*) turns warm gold in dry periods. Muhly grass (*Muhlenbergia capillaris*) and purple love grass (*Eragrostis spectabilis*) can rival any perennial for color with their airy pink-red inflorescences in late summer. Indiangrass (*Sorghastrum nutans*) stays low and green through spring and early summer, then shoots up and produces feathery plumes with tiny orange and gold accents.

Dryland gardeners have a rich palette of succulents available to them that other gardeners envy. Succulents exude a special charisma. Their sturdy forms give an impression of abundance that belies the dry environment, maybe because we know they are holding water. From tiny *Crassula pubescens*, with its creamy flowers on red stems rising from a mat of leaves under 6 inches, to towering 20-foot *Aloe barberae*, succulent plants take a variety of shapes and sizes. Their skins are nearly every hue of the rainbow, including pink-tipped *Euphorbia tirucalli* 'Sticks on Fire', dark orange *Kalanchoe luciae*, and the beloved blue groundcover *Senecio serpens*.

Trees are perhaps more important to people's comfort in arid regions than elsewhere. Even if they don't directly shade your house—and many dry-climate trees won't get tall enough to do this in a person's lifetime—they create zones of cooler air around your home, which can significantly affect your indoor and outdoor comfort. They also provide life-giving shade for shorter plants, protecting them from desiccation and adding rare organic matter to the soil. They can be ornamental as well as useful; consider the iridescent green-trunked palo verde (*Parkinsonia aculeata*) and its relatives. Many desert trees produce exceptionally fragrant flowers, including Texas ebony tree (*Ebenopsis ebano*), winter-flowering sweet acacia (*A. farnesiana*), and the smaller guajillo (*Acacia berlandieri*). With their picturesque, convoluted forms and the cave-like shelter they promise, desert trees can be the most evocative elements in your landscape.

Dry-adapted verbenas, salvias, and penstemons bloom on the slope above a courtyard.

An urban front yard holds more succulents than you can count, including Caribbean agave (A. angustifolia *var.* marginata*), furcraea, and several charismatic golden barrel cacti (*Echinocactus grusonii*).*

stylin' hardscapes

In arid areas throughout the West and Southwest, gardeners and landscape designers are experimenting with and perfecting ways to make visually stunning gardens that rely more on hardscape and less on ill-adapted plantings. They are using bold hardscape elements—local rock in particular, but also adobe, crushed rock, glass beads, brick, and repurposed concrete—supplemented with a diverse blend of dry-adapted plants, for a modern look that appeals to all our senses. They are harnessing the cooling power of rock walls, shaded rock patios, and the microclimates created by well-placed trees to build comfortable havens for people.

A waterwise garden can still have a water feature. Minimalist plantings keep the focus on the grand architecture, while the pond conveys cooled air to a shaded outdoor dining room.

One recently installed lawnless front garden in Boise, Idaho, features a locally quarried andesite path with a central patio. Jason Doran of Willowglenn Landscape ranged groups of perennials around the hardscape and along the boulevard—dry-adapted plants (*Sedum reflexum*, *S. rupestre*, *Yucca filamentosa* 'Color Guard') rubbing shoulders with drought-tolerant woodland varieties (*Heuchera* 'Velvet Night', *Lamium maculatum* 'Pink Pewter', *Carex oshimensis* 'Evergold'). "I wanted to

Large rocks with the patina of age add year-round character to a dryland parking lot. Fast-growing trees give summer shade, and assorted grasses add movement and life to the cityscape.

show that a water-thrifty landscape can be created using plants not generally associated with xeric gardens," says Jason. Unlike the surrounding lawns, which must be watered every couple of days, this xeric garden needs only infrequent irrigation. Highly efficient rotary stream nozzles combined with careful plant selection and placement have given the homeowners an 80 percent water savings over their old lawn.

Elsewhere in Boise, an Albertsons grocery store has joined the regional landscaping trend with gusto, converting all the islands in their extensive parking lot to dry-adapted plants mulched with gravel and decorated with large, lichen-encrusted boulders. Not only do boulders shade the soil, slowing evaporation and retaining moisture, but they can also bring water into an arid garden, condensing it onto their night-cooled surfaces as the morning air heats up around them. Placed under the canopies of plants, they catch and magnify the water vapor that the plants release, creating a moister microclimate. And like other hardscape elements, they make interesting scenery, especially during the winter.

regional resonance

In their large suburban Colorado backyard, garden designers and authors Lauren Springer Ogden and Scott Ogden have made an inviting, comfortable garden with elements that are at home in this arid intermountain region. Low, grass-dominated expanses reminiscent of shortgrass prairie, steppe, and spring-fed meadow flow across the backyard. Several copses of trees and shrubs are carefully sited to screen views of buildings and increase the perceived size of the garden. These also add four-season vertical structure that a strict grassland lacks.

From the back door, a stone path wanders out into the garden, to a fire pit encircled by low stone benches. Many paths lead away from this central seating area. Enfolded by an arm of mounded rockery, it beckons people into the garden, promising a human-friendly place from which to venture out and explore the wilder surroundings. The open landscape around the fire pit offers long views across the garden as well as glimpses of distant shrub- and grass-covered foothills that rise up between the neighboring homes. It's a perfect spot in which to linger and soak up the calm of the subtly colored, subtly shifting grasses and their less abundant but more vivid floral companions. In *Plant-Driven Design*, the Ogdens write, "What its indoor cousin the hearth is to a house, the fire pit is to our garden: the heart and center where plants, stone, sky, fire, friends, and family can all come together."

Admittedly, theirs is a gardener's garden that required broad knowledge of plants to create and demands skilled stewardship as well. Its authentic look comes from understanding and emulating the region in which it is located.

But although the garden looks natural, plants are not allowed to grow or spread uncontrolled. The Ogdens water some areas during the growing season when there is less than an inch of rainfall per month; they monitor this as their climate is prone to irregular droughts. Though very few weeds have come into the garden, it requires a significant amount of time and effort to pull or dig out self-sown seedlings of their happy plants. In the shortest planting areas, they clip off the seedheads of several self-sowing grasses as soon as they bloom to keep them from overwhelming their less prolific fellows. And once a year in late winter, they go through the grassy areas and cut down all the grasses and perennials.

While this diverse yet serene landscape demands informed intervention, it needs no fertilizers or pesticides, no lawn mower, no soil amendment, and very little irrigation. Drought-tolerant grasses, sedges, and perennials make up the bulk of the plantings. The thousands of bulbs that bring a brief colorful show in early spring take advantage of extra water delivered during that season in this climate, and of a natural swale that channels more of this spring bounty to them when it's most appreciated. And the Ogdens are rewarded with dynamic changes through the seasons and even throughout each day; visual, aural, and textural delights; and of course fresh inspiration and a testing ground for new designs.

top: The regional resonance of a natural stone and grassland garden, home of garden designers Lauren Springer Ogden and Scott Ogden, makes a comfortable place for relaxing in the wilds of a Colorado suburb.

bottom: Scattered clusters of grasses catch and release the early morning sun in the Ogdens' dry-adapted suburban backyard.

edible gardens

Peas, perfect for snacking
as you wander through your
garden.

W hether you are committed to seasonal local eating or just want to be able to pluck sun-warmed cherry tomatoes from the vine and pop them into your mouth, growing food can be a rewarding experience. Homegrown food is not only extra delicious but extra healthy too. Plant foods contain antioxidants and other volatile but essential nutrients that start to dissipate as soon as they are harvested. The longer these foods are stored, the lower their nutritional value. The chance to eat more homegrown produce or to use freshly picked herbs in daily kitchen creations has compelled many cooks to become gardeners.

Edible crops delight more than just our sense of taste. Their aromas infuse a garden; for instance, the smell of ripe, sun-warmed grapes can carry over a mile. Most food plants have been bred for generations, developing a wide array of varieties. Each might have a distinct flavor, as well as different colors on the leaves, pods, flowers, and stems, and perhaps even the interiors.

Certain annual vegetables need ongoing care and specialized knowledge to grow. However, many herbs thrive without care if they are sited well. You can save money by growing your favorite herbs; often one plant can supply your needs for many meals through the year, and will cost less than buying one meal's supply from the grocery store. If you plan to use an herb in quantity for tea, canning, or herbal crafts, growing it can be cost-effective and convenient.

Edible gardens should include companion plants, for added beauty and for their useful contributions: pollen for pollinators, habitat for pest predators, and soil-building nutrients. If you want the most reward for the least work, plant perennial food plants. They may need a few seasons (or longer) to become established and productive, but your investment of time and effort will be repaid with easy, abundant food sources that bear for decades.

More food gardeners are beginning to incorporate animals into their gardens. From bees and earthworms to goats and chickens, animals can have a profound beneficial effect on a food garden. They help to cycle nutrients, control pests, boost productivity, and speed decomposition. They produce foods such as eggs, honey, and milk, which round out the plant-based offerings of the garden. (Some animals are prohibited or regulated in urban residential areas; consult your city zoning laws for the latest ordinances—gardeners have successfully revised many of them!)

Food brings people together. Growing food creates opportunities to learn, work, share, and meet kindred spirits. Edible gardens create enjoyable moments for children as well as adults; herbs, fruits, and vegetables produce snacks for grazing, and flowers bring fragrance, butterflies, and color into the yard. Discovering new food plants, growing them in artistic combinations, and sampling their flavors makes a rewarding multisensory pastime that can be pursued with friends and the entire family.

urban food farm

The home gardens of Minneapolis landscape designer and permaculturist Paula Westmoreland demonstrate how much food can be grown in an urban setting, even in a cold climate.

It may not be obvious to the casual visitor, but Paula's front yard is a perennial food garden. Woolly thyme (*Thymus pseudolanuginosus*) covers bare ground and deters windblown weeds, and clumps of chives (*Allium schoenoprasum*) give a long season of edible greens and attract pollinators for two pear trees and a currant bush; it all looks like a naturalistic but well-kept woodland garden. And her sunny backyard, split between a patio and an edible garden, reflects the fundamental goals of permaculture: making places for people to live comfortably outdoors as well as growing useful plants in eco-friendly ways that promote soil health, human health, and functional ecological communities.

The central keyhole bed of annual and perennial vegetables, herbs, and flowers is irrigated with drip hoses hidden under a light layer of mulch. Its horseshoe shape is well suited to smaller gardens, with maximum planting area and minimal space taken by paths. It also lets you reach all the plants for tending and harvesting. Keyhole beds can be sized to fit into a square or circular space, or they can be laid out side by side to fill a long narrow space. They can be created around trees, mini-ponds, bean teepees, or other central features.

Dotted around Paula's keyhole bed are other beds of various sizes and shapes, each holding a suite of plants that grow well together. There are blueberry bushes with a ground layer of bunchberry (*Cornus canadensis*), an asparagus bed with a living mulch of sweet alyssum (*Lobularia maritima*), an herb spiral, a potato tower, several islands of assorted high-nectar perennials to attract pollinators and other beneficial insects, and stands of heirloom garlic.

Two cold frames allow Paula to harvest fresh greens and early crops while the soil in the rest of the garden is still too cold for active plant growth. Associated maintenance is minimal; their plantings need supplemental water now and then, but the main work is opening the

Vegetables, herbs, and flowers grown together make a food garden more colorful and more productive.

Paula Westmoreland's lawnless urban backyard allows space for growing edibles and for eating them.

The keyhole bed just after it was built.

Every year, the keyhole bed nurtures a new mix of edibles and ornamentals, all within easy reach.

Cold frames extend the short northern growing season and protect young greens from that ubiquitous urban predator, the rabbit.

lids when the sun shines to keep the plants from over-heating and wilting, then closing the lids at night or in colder weather to keep the temperature warm enough inside. This could be automated by installing self-opening hinges; they use liquid-filled cylinders that expand and contract as the temperature changes.

Having customers with limited space, Paula is always experimenting with new ways to fit more plants (especially edibles) into small urban settings, including green roofs. Diversity and soil health are crucial. "We need to work with nature," she says. "It's more sustainable and cost-effective than working against it."

front and center

After their successful backyard renovation, California retirees Roy and Rosadelia Detwiler replaced their front lawn too. Their eye-catching new front garden makes the case that edibles can be grown in plain sight and still appeal to even the tidiest among us.

Designer Kelly Marshall, who created the Detwilers' back landscape as well, gave this edible garden a formal structure for year-round presence. Raised stone beds, paths of decomposed granite, and a central urn with a fountain beautify the property and neighborhood in all seasons. Permanent living structures include a hedge of blueberry (*Vaccinium*) and rosemary (*Rosmarinus*) shrubs and a bed of espaliered pear trees underplanted with strawberries. Roy and Rosadelia have received a lot of positive comments about the garden's design from neighbors and visitors, many of whom don't realize at first that it includes food plants.

The raised beds make it easier to harvest the plants and to plan the crop rotation for vegetables. Three of these beds are replanted annually with tomatoes, eggplants, lettuce, various chilies, zucchini, tomatillos, pumpkins, potatoes, broccoli, and cauliflower. The fourth is devoted to perennial herbs including mint, three kinds of oregano, parsley, sage, thyme, lemon balm, chives, and manzanilla (*Matricaria recutita*) for teas. Separating out the perennials makes it easy to perform more intensive maintenance and successive planting in the annual beds without damaging the soil and root structure of the perennials.

The Detwilers often pick food in their front yard and cook and eat it in their backyard. Their garden produces enough to share, so their fortunate neighbors get a beautiful view and fresh food too!

This edible garden features four raised stone beds surrounding a bubbling central fountain.

top: Savory structures: an evergreen rosemary hedge (Rosmarinus officinalis 'Athens Blue Spires') and an espaliered pear (Pyrus).

bottom: Raised beds bring the plants up to you, making it easier to pick, snap, sort, and sit admiring the harvest.

going vertical

One way to fit more edibles into a small space is to grow them vertically. Generations of vegetable gardeners have rigged up all kinds of growing structures, using whatever materials they had on hand. Annual pea vines can grow up sticks that are sunk into the ground, or pieces of string hanging from one horizontal support. If you already have a fence, many vines or sprawling plants can be trained up it. For grapes (*Vitis*), hardy kiwis (*Actinidia kolomikta*), passionfruit (*Passiflora edulis*), and other perennial vines, it is worth erecting an arbor or other permanent structure... but if you don't have the skill or the funds, don't worry. The plants will grow either way. Even squashes and melons can be trained up trellises; tie them at intervals, using strips of cloth or lengths of rope or twine, but avoid using uncoated wire as it can damage or snap their tender stalks.

An herb spiral is an easy and ingenious design for growing a variety of herbs that need different conditions within a small space together, and giving you easy access to all the plants for harvesting. Start with a mound of soil at least 3 feet across. Use good soil, with a light structure and high in organic matter, to give your plants a quick start and years of healthy growth. Settle the soil by watering the mound thoroughly before planting. Slightly flatten the soil to make level planting space, starting on top of the mound and winding down around it in a spiral. A border of rocks around the edge of the flattened area will increase your spiral's visual appeal and help retain soil too. At the bottom, you can dig a shallow basin and let your spiral curl around it like a cat's tail.

Plant herbs along the spiral, choosing places that best fit each plant's preferences. The optional basin makes a good site for moisture-tolerant herbs such as dill and parsley, or if you have a larger area, horseradish. The well-drained sites at the top of the mound are good for herbs that cannot abide wet feet; shorter thymes and oreganos can be placed on the sunniest side, with taller lavender and rosemary behind. On the north slope, where earth and other plants block the hottest sun, grow herbs that tend to bolt or scorch in the heat, such as coriander and the delectable, lemony perennial sorrel *Rumex acetosa* 'Profusion', which does not go to seed like other varieties.

For this small-space design, it is best to avoid herbs that spread indefinitely. In general, plants that need more territory (running plants like mints and self-sowers such as feverfew) should be sited in larger areas where they can grow naturally without making extra work for the gardener. Set aside a patch of land and grow them all together, or you can curtail their vigorous growth by planting the running herbs in pots sunk into the ground, and clipping off the flowerheads of self-sowers before they set seed.

Paula Westmoreland and her cohorts at Ecological Gardens have invented an easy, inexpensive structure for growing food vertically. They make potato towers for their clients' gardens using 3-foot-high sturdy metal fencing. To make your own, cut a length of fencing and loop it to form a cylinder. Stand it in the garden with an open end facing up. Choose a location that is partly sunny but not too hot, with good air circulation. Paula advises filling your tower with 100 percent compost to avoid potato blight. The tricky part is to get the compost evenly moist before you plant; she has used a hose to trickle water down the center for up to eight hours to achieve this.

Plant your potato starts a few inches deep, up and down the sides of the tower. If you used fine-weave fencing, you may need to cut holes in the sides so you can reach in to plant. For smaller potatoes, plant the starts closer together. Paula says, "It's fun to mix varieties—we often mix French fingerling, Peruvian purple potato, and Yukon gold." The potatoes will grow out the sides and top, covering the structure to make a leafy green tower. Good companion plants are nasturtiums, which have spicy, edible leaves and flowers and attract predator insects. Paula uses them to help provide shade down the

top: An herb spiral at its prime in late summer.

bottom: A potato tower is an effective way to grow potatoes in a small space.

side of the bin and keep the compost from drying out, but she cautions not to let the nasturtiums shade out the potatoes. When you are ready to harvest the potatoes, tip over the bin, or separate the edges and pull it open.

Another vertical strategy is to make a teepee with several posts tied together at the top or "capped" with a clay pot. Peas can be planted around the outside and lettuce within, and as the season warms, the developing shade of the peas will keep the lettuces cooler so they produce longer.

beneficial companions

If you spread your food plants out and intersperse them with beneficial companion plants, your garden will hold fewer "productive" plants, but they will need less help to grow and produce. A diversity of plants will host a diversity of insects, which will attract a diversity of insect predators—and all the different populations will keep each other in check. If you diversify your crops, then even if disease, drought, hard rains, or early frost decimate some of your plants, you will still get a harvest.

Flowers that have flat, broad "landing pads" attract pollinators, which will increase your harvest. Herbs such as dill and fennel have these pollen-rich flowers, as do ornamental perennials like yarrow. Aim to keep something blooming at all times throughout the growing season. If pollinators can always find pollen or nectar in your garden, they can live there year-round, and they will be available when your fruits or vegetables need their service. Your garden will be colorful and interesting to you during the entire growing season too.

Some plants attract insects that eat other insects, and these insect predators will help keep less desirable bugs in check so you won't need to use poisons. For example, white clover (*Trifolium repens*) attracts parasitoid wasps, which are tiny (too tiny to sting people) insects that lay their eggs on other insects, including many that are con-

sidered garden pests. When the wasp larvae hatch, they eat their insect host.

Every plant produces chemical compounds as a defense against predators or as a byproduct of its growth. Nitrogen-fixing plants—alfalfa, clovers, legumes like peas and beans—convert atmospheric nitrogen to a form that other plants can use. They make beneficial companions because plants need nitrogen for healthy growth. Nitrogen fixers can be grown among your other plants, or they can be cut and the clippings spread around for a mild natural fertilizer.

Some plants are useful companions for the minerals they concentrate in their tissues. Dandelions, for instance, have long taproots that seek out calcium that may be too deep in the soil for other plants to reach; when they die (or are pulled and left to decompose in the garden), the stored calcium is returned to the surface of the soil, where it can be used by soil microorganisms and, eventually, other plants. Dandelions are edibles, too, and a good source of calcium for people.

Plants with large, dense clusters of leaves at the base of their stems can shade the ground in your vegetable garden and prevent weeds. Comfrey (*Symphytum*) is such a plant; it grows densely enough to outcompete most ground-layer plants, and because it too accumulates nutrients in its tissues, it makes a great self-mulching understory for young fruit trees that need extra nutrition. It can be cut and its leaves added to compost or laid around other plants, where it will decompose and boost the nutrient content of the soil. (Just don't move any little pieces of the root anywhere that you don't want to have comfrey growing forever.)

With a variety of companion plants interspersed among your food plants, not only will your edible garden be healthier, but it will also be more beautiful and more lively, with diverse colors and creatures all through the growing season. And plenty of good food too.

Nitrogen fixers milkvetch (Astragalus, foreground) and sweetpea (Lathyrus, midground) enrich the soil and contribute to the healthy growth of other plants.

growing community

LeRoy Gonsior lives in a small town in Minnesota. His backyard food garden—visible from the street and from other yards in this fenceless neighborhood—is just like the ones that stood beside many farmhouses in previous generations. Flowers bloom alongside edibles as they have ever since LeRoy's grandfather started the garden in 1926.

Though he has enlarged it over the years, LeRoy still maintains the garden using techniques his parents taught him. He plants his pepper seedlings in cut-off milk cartons to keep cutworms from chewing through their tender stems. He mulches his vegetable and fruit plants with grass clippings from his own lawn and those of neighbors who don't use lawn chemicals. In one corner of the garden he collects food waste in a large compost pile all year. Every fall he distributes the processed compost over the garden, along with a foot-deep layer of leaves from neighborhood trees, and rototills it in.

And LeRoy rototills again every spring. Despite this, he says, "If you go out into the garden with a pitchfork in the spring, you can dig up one forkful of dirt and have a hundred earthworms in it." In fact, his earthworms could be considered something of a menace, for instance when they pulled a good portion of his newly planted onion seedlings underground one night after he planted them. But he has perfected his own technique for protecting onions: now he saves some leaves each fall and uses them to mulch around the onion seedlings, and the worms eat the leaves instead.

Food-growing strategies may take years of experience and experiments, and they are often site-specific; what works in LeRoy's garden may not work in yours. In generations past, grandparents and parents would hand down time-tested techniques to children who remained in or near the family home, but this happens rarely nowadays. We move every few years on average, and some of us rent

Dahlias and eggplants bloom side by side in LeRoy Gonsior's kitchen garden.

our properties or belong to an association that manages or limits our landscaping. With more of us working outside the home, we may not have the time to grow food.

But all that is changing. Environmentalists and locavores are lauding local foods as a fun and effective way to lower your carbon footprint and improve your health while helping to build a thriving community. A new generation of vegetable gardeners is relearning the art of growing vegetables the way our grandparents or great-grandparents did: on a small scale, using manual tech-

A bench invites you to relish the visual feast spread out across LeRoy Gonsior's backyard.

niques, and with a shoestring budget. Students of all ages are getting both lessons and meals from edible schoolyard gardens they have designed and built. Restaurants are noticing it is more efficient and better for business to plan seasonal menus, growing some of their food supply or contracting with local farmers. Cities and towns are setting aside vacant lots for use as community gardens. And we all are eating healthier because of it.

If you don't happen to have a parent or grandparent handy to teach you about growing food in your yard, you could befriend an experienced food gardener in your neighborhood, church, or other circle of acquaintances. Many will be glad to have an "apprentice," and you can help out in exchange for learning techniques that can save you a lot of work and frustration in your own garden. You may even find more ways to cooperate, such as growing different crops and then exchanging some with your new garden mentor, or canning your harvests together. Other places to find garden mentors and gain hands-on experience include local community gardens and Community Supported Agriculture (CSA) farms; in exchange for your work you will get a great education, a network of garden friends, and you will eat well too.

stroll gardens

One glance is not enough, nor likely is one visit, when the setting offers a deft balance of open spaces and partial views.

Some gardens, not necessarily larger in size, are designed to encompass more plants, more experiences, more feet of walking path, and more all-around variety. These stroll gardens are made for exploring. You cannot take them in at one glance, maybe not even during one visit. And if you are so lucky or clever as to have one in your yard, you will find yourself drawn outdoors in all weather, at all hours, just to see what is happening.

From a pathside resting place to an open eating area, to a contemplative room with a distant view, to a reflecting pool or fountain, your stroll garden can give you the space for a whole range of experiences. Use eye-level barriers to mask part of the view and pique curiosity. Embrace (or invent) rough terrain, as it focuses the attention on the experience of moving through the garden. Add surprises where you can, to enhance the garden's mystery and the garden visitor's sense of adventurous exploration.

A cottage garden could be considered a condensed stroll garden. It favors flowers over open space and could be the best style if you have a very small yard and want a lot of color. It's also a good choice for artists. Besides bringing cheer, it will give ample blooms for cutting, painting, or photography. Cottage gardens can be economical to install and

Southern hospitality flourishes in this generous front yard cottage garden.

maintain. You can use dependable, old-fashioned flowers grown from seed or bought in flats, or purchase annuals in bulk. The design can be very simple, just a path or two through the yard, which is planted densely with a mix of whatever plants you enjoy or can grow.

Cottage and stroll gardens are for people who scan a pristine green lawn and feel not a spark of interest, people who stop the car when they spot an unfamiliar bloom or bug, hikers and cyclists, bird and butterfly enthusiasts. They are for people who take pleasure in being surrounded by plants and animals, who cannot just look at a landscape but really must leap into it.

streamside explorer's garden

Sharon and Jim Holman share a love of plants and nature, so they worked with local landscape architect and ecologist Diane Hilscher to create an extensive stroll garden that would add significant wildlife habitat to their property in Stillwater, Minnesota.

The central feature of the garden is a built stream that flows from an upper pond next to their deck down to a lower pond where the garden meets the driveway. Carefully placed rocks create naturalistic rills and eddies, and the sound of moving water carries through their open windows day and night, giving their home and garden a profoundly soothing quality. The ever-moving stream is a foil to the two ponds, which are centers of deep stillness in the garden. Sitting on the deck, you can soak in this calm as you survey your surroundings.

Glancing downstream from the upper pond, your eyes might linger on the inviting stone bridge. It crosses the stream and merges into a pea gravel path that branches and curves as it leads explorers through the garden. Views are concealed, then vistas revealed, as the path meanders around large, dense shrubs and up and down along the hillside. Sharon and Jim keep the tall trees limbed up so that a variety of ground-layer plants can thrive, from woodland natives in the deeper pockets of shade to low-growing sun-lovers alongside the paths. Each area and mood gradually transitions to the next, making the landscape feel as natural as possible. The patio outside the front door is a veritable who's-who of charming groundcovers, including multiple species of violets and sedums in tones of gray-blue and purple. Those that can't take as much foot traffic are tucked into protected pockets between rocks.

As you explore, you are sure to spot plenty of animals. The watery elements provide bathing and drinking areas for birds, dragonflies, and frogs. Native grasses and flowers supply pollen, nectar, seeds, butterfly larval food, and

top left: Comfortably settled on an easy-care living carpet of deadnettle (Lamium maculatum), a bench surveys the front steps, planted patio, stone bridge, and a path that wanders off into the garden.

bottom left: Stream and staircase descend the hill together.

top right: A birch (Betula) presides over an island of ground-layer plants, including epimediums, jack-in-the-pulpit (Arisaema), maidenhair fern (Adiantum pedatum), and Japanese forest grass (Hakonechloa macra 'Aureola').

bottom right: Diverse plantings and moving water attract both wildlife and people.

nesting materials. A mix of understory trees and shrubs offer nesting sites and perches, and the groundcovers throughout are tall enough to shield frogs as they travel through the garden and in and out of the ponds.

The Holmans used to spend three hours each time they mowed their extensive lawn. Now, with no lawn, the bulk of their yardwork involves weed control, which is not nearly as frequent or urgent. They use chemicals to keep the paths clear for strolling, and when they have the time, they hand- or spot-weed dandelions and tree seedlings that pop up in the ground-layer plantings. Freed from lawn maintenance, Sharon and Jim have enjoyed adding their own creative touches to the garden for nearly a decade. Together they have designed and built several copper structures for their climbing plants, and Jim has created sculptural cairns, which make a textural contrast against the plant foliage during the growing season and lend a reassuring, solid structure year-round. This wildlife habitat garden has become prime human habitat too.

many rooms, many moods

At the center of Jeremy and Amy-Ann Mayberg's garden is a circular patio with a fire pit. While relaxing there, you can enjoy views into two shade gardens, a mini-prairie, and a pond garden. These glimpses into the surrounding areas invite you to choose one of the curving paths that wander away from the patio. Fire or water, shade or sun, solitude or society: whatever you're in the mood for, this urban backyard delivers.

The plants in the mini-prairie grow tall enough to fill most of the view when you are seated around the fire pit, but standing up, you can see across them to the woodland garden beyond. A flagstone path arcs through the prairie. Designer Erik James Olsen of Out Back Nursery, Hastings, Minnesota, shaped this path to suggest the movement of the wind. Wind is an ever-present element in an open expanse of natural prairie, but it does not sweep through urban neighborhoods in the same way, and he wanted to bring its echo into the garden.

Most of the plants in the mini-prairie are native to the region. Grasses dominate; little bluestem (*Schizachyrium scoparium*) and prairie dropseed (*Sporobolus heterolepis*) provide the main grass layer, with shorter oak sedge (*Carex pensylvanica*) filling in alongside the path and under the taller plants. The flowers, less numerous, are specially chosen for showiness and to have something beautiful blooming in every part of the growing season. Amy-Ann adores the "troll-head tufts" of prairie smoke (*Geum triflorum*), while Jeremy is partial to rough blazingstars (*Liatris aspera*), which he ties to inconspicuous stakes so their torch-like blooms are held upright and visible above the grasses in midsummer. Mat-forming pussytoes (*Antennaria neglecta*) runs among the cracks between the stones and forms colonies along parts of the path, stitching it to the planting area; feeling plants underfoot creates a more powerful experience of walking through, rather than alongside, the garden.

Another path off the fire pit patio leads to a gravel garden with a rectangular pond. Thick hydrangeas and arborvitaes along two sides and a solitary bench invite quiet contemplation. The burbling water attracts birds. Though you can see back along the path to the fire pit patio, the main view is a woodland with a low understory of mostly native groundcovers, dominated by a mature river birch (*Betula nigra*). The simplicity of design and the sparseness of elements within this garden room bring a real sense of peace. Here is a haven, a respite from the "too much" and "too fast" of the outside world.

From this pondering garden, a path of round stepping stones leads through the adjacent woodland toward the house. As you walk you can glimpse, through the birch foliage, the open clearing made up of patio and prairie. This makes your exploration somewhat private without wholly isolating you from what is going on in the "hub."

left: The fire pit patio is the "hub" of this garden, and paths of different materials promise a variety of experiences.

right: The mood is lively in the circular mini-prairie, and its proximity to the patio makes it easy to admire visiting butterflies.

Prairie smoke (Geum triflorum) flowers, which look like tiny dark pink rosehips, metamorphose into feathery seedheads after pollination.

For peaceful repose, nothing beats a bench, a pond, and a woodland garden.

The "civilized" concrete patio is on the left; "nature" awaits, on the right.

The only lawn in the yard is a small path that connects the fire pit patio to another concrete patio just off the house. This patio is the most "civilized" space in the garden, good for brief forays outdoors or more formal gatherings, where people may not be dressed to mingle closely with nature or to walk across less-than-even pavement.

This 90- by 35-foot garden's low ground-layer plants and its separate spaces keep the openness and visibility some of us love about our lawns while making it easier to find a place to suit a certain mood or activity. Jeremy says, "We particularly like sitting in the shade at the western edge of the garden, looking east across a sunny prairie into a shaded woodland beyond. The woodland may be on the other side of the garden, but it's so very easy to imagine yourself on a back-forty somewhere. I can't imagine a better view, a more restful place, and it's constantly changing."

The diversity of spaces and the well-chosen plants in this urban stroll garden also have a lot to offer wildlife. Plants are predominantly native to the region, making an ideal environment for local animals with a shared history of co-evolution. Different ecological communities—woodland, prairie, and pond—attract a greater variety of animal species. The garden's trees and mixed shrubs provide nesting sites, cover, and food for birds, and the pond offers them a site for drinking and bathing. And the prairie is a butterfly magnet, especially when the blazing-stars are blooming.

fragrant cottage garden

Over the past 20 years, on half their double city lot in Saint Paul, Marilyn and Harold Buss have built a garden that is the stuff of dreams. In true cottage style, their garden bursts with bloom from spring to fall, and its dramatically changeful show, visible from the street through a screen of foliage above a short white picket fence, lures many a passerby to peer into its depths and sigh with bliss.

The garden's earliest display comes from the "tapestry hedge" of different spring-flowering shrubs, which heralds warm weather with painterly pastels and the rich scents of lilac (*Syringa vulgaris*) and yellow-flowered clove currant (*Ribes odoratum*). This blooming hedge peeks out from under several mature maples, which shade the southern half of the garden from the afternoon sun. Under the maples, Marilyn grows fragrant violets (*Viola*), lily-of-the-valley (*Convallaria majalis*), Virginia bluebells (*Mertensia virginica*), and ferns.

Go ahead. Peek through the white lattice, and you'll be catapulted out of the city.

Iris, roses, and peonies provide a second wave of color, and the stars of Marilyn's garden begin to send up their green spires in early summer. They are a convivial crowd of garden phlox (*P. paniculata*), which by July are swelling across the open areas of the garden and around the trunks of several fruit trees, a sweetly scented sea of pink, white, and lavender blossoms. Here and there, other plants—ultra-tall double sunflowers (*Helianthus ×multiflorus* 'Flore Pleno'), spiked speedwell (*Veronica spicata*)—add spots of vivid color. In the sunniest corner of the garden are hollyhocks (*Alcea rosea*), self-sowing biennials that pop up in new places each year. Their dramatic spires tower taller than a person, displaying pink, red, white, and yellow flowers at eye level like friendly faces, greeting you as you pause to savor their bold floral flavors.

You enter the garden by stepping under a wooden arbor, painted white to match the picket fence. A looping path leads you past a half-hidden bench and a playhouse, across an open meadow. You are hip-deep in color all late summer, and by summer's end the path is nearly hidden by stems arching under the weight of flowers.

Marilyn and Harold have developed a straightforward and not overly demanding routine to keep their floral companions thriving and spreading. She waters whenever the weather is dry, using tall copper sprinklers that broadcast water above the heads of the tall perennials. He moves the sprinklers around for her and spends a couple of summer days on a ladder pruning the trees. She weeds the gravel paths manually. And every fall they spend a couple of days together, cutting down the plants and putting the garden to bed. It is always a sad time. "It's funny how emotional you get over a garden," Marilyn says. Luckily, they have many months' memories of abundant bloom to carry them through the long Minnesota winters.

*As the phlox begin to fade, yellow accents of brown-eyed susan (*Rudbeckia triloba*) pepper this urban meadow.*

144

a story garden

Kelly Stevens has a story for everything, and so does her southern garden. She taught herself to read and write as an adult, but she grew up using storytelling as a primary means of remembering and communicating. Her ability to see the story in each object has led to an eclectic mix in her home landscape. She spots a plant, or a bit of metal trellis, or an old teakettle, and has an immediate vision for how it could be included in her garden. For example, she snapped up a marked-down redbud (*Cercis canadensis* 'Forest Pansy') for its heart-shaped leaves that emerge red, like valentines, every spring. The half-dead tree became the centerpiece of a garden room honoring her mother's memory. It thrives, like everything else in the garden, thanks to Kelly's skills and determination.

The garden's several distinct "rooms" cover most of Kelly's urban yard. An outdoor living room holds a padded swinging bench, several mismatched chairs, a small pond, and a fountain. One sunny room holds a central bog garden in an old bathtub and a row of old garden tools placed like sculptures along one border. Beside that is an open graveled area with a sturdy cast concrete table and benches, set in a circle of white stone; the gravel areas were established by smothering the lawn with old plastic bags from mulch, potting soil, and other materials Kelly uses when landscaping her clients' gardens.

Lacking the funds to spend on outdoor décor, Kelly sticks to bargains and found objects. She also barters her services as a landscape designer, builder, rock worker, and plain old laborer. Her garden is a labor of love in which plants are kept trimmed and tidy and objects arranged just so. It might appear to be "full of junk," as Kelly sheepishly describes it, but a person need not spend long there before realizing that it is full of character and history. Just like its gardener.

top left: This whimsical garden is furnished with discarded items, clearance merchandise, traded materials, and "extras" contributed by friends, family, and a few kind strangers.

bottom left: Early morning light moves quickly across the garden. At back center is the redbud tree.

top right: A standing stone and large metal cross mark a memorial to the gardener's mother.

bottom right: A grove of golden bamboo (Phyllostachys aurea) encircles this outdoor room. It is limbed up to show off its bright culms and let more light in.

The garden wall that borders this private "memory lane" includes a handmade mosaic memorializing the destruction of New York City's Twin Towers.

smarter lawns

If you want to keep a lawn—and many of us do—you can make one that will take substantially less water, time, and work than the "ideal" perfect lawn. Though it won't look like a golf course, it might still satisfy the needs of your family for an open and usable patch of green.

It is a one-time chore and expense to convert your thirsty turf to a lawn made of low and slow-growing species, and the savings in time and money will just keep accruing. While the average high-performance, high-demand lawn needs to be cut 25 to 40 times a year and fertilized one to four times a year, most low and slow species need zero to four annual mowings and grow best without fertilizer. Imagine all the new memories you can make, many of them outdoors, in those precious summer hours that you no longer spend tending your lawn.

In the arid Southwest, pink-purple torches of blazingstar (Liatris) liven up a low front lawn of native, dry-adapted blue grama (Bouteloua gracilis) and spike muhly (Muhlenbergia wrightii) grasses.

You could also put less effort into your existing lawn, transitioning it to a freedom lawn that includes white and red clover, trefoil, violets, dock, and other broadleaf plants, or letting it grow up into a managed meadow that needs only occasional care but could become a lawn again at times when you need one.

You may wonder, what would the neighbors think? Their lives might be improved as well. Instead of smelling your lawnmower fumes, they would be smelling your honeysuckle. Instead of standing on their porch swatting the bugs you've attracted with your well-watered turf, they could be cuddled up on their porch swing enjoying a bug-free desert sunset. Their fruit trees will bear bumper crops, thanks to the pollinators you support with your high-nectar freedom lawn. Silencing your leaf-blower will allow them (and you) to hear the calls of neighborhood birds. They too might appreciate the backlit inflorescences of your managed meadow, and after dark, the bobbing of fireflies.

low and slow

Some grasses and grass-like plants have a mature size of 6 inches or lower. Others grow slowly to an eventual size of 12 to 16 inches but arch over after their blades reach a certain length, forming a rolling, ankle-deep carpet. All can be kept lower if desired, by mowing just a few times a year. Few are suited to heavy foot traffic or high-intensity recreational use.

In general, lawns made with low and slow-growing species require more time and care at the beginning compared to seeded Kentucky bluegrass or quick-spreading bermudagrass, but once established, they demand significantly less water, little or no fertilizer, and little or no mowing. What's more, some can grow well (with the same low level of care) in areas where traditional sun-loving turfgrasses do poorly. If you are putting in a lawn from scratch, and if you won't be using it for ball games or a dog run, low and slow is the way to go. It may take some research up front but will save you money and effort in the long run. This also applies if you are willing to kill off your lawn and start over, as part of making your landscape more comfortable and easier to care for.

The first step is to figure out which low and slow species will grow with minimal care in your location. No matter where you live, you will find several to dozens of species that are well suited to your climate. (Your site, on the other hand, may not be suited for growing a low and slow lawn—or any lawn at all—if the land is too steep or too shaded, or if the soil is too shallow or too waterlogged. In these cases, you might try a living carpet, a woodland garden, a xeric garden, or a rain garden, respectively.)

In the cool temperate regions of the United States and Canada, blends of non-native fine fescues (*Festuca*) make a low-care turf. These grasses need sandy or loamy soil and are not suitable for consistently wet soil or clay. They generally grow well in part shade to full sun. They grow

The "hill and valley" texture of a no-mow mixed fescue lawn invites you to sit or lie down on its billowy, pillowy surface.

best without supplemental water or fertilizer, though you may need to irrigate infrequently but deeply during dry, hot summers if you want them to stay green. A fescue lawn can be kept at a 4-inch height with two to four mowings per year, or it can be cut once a year (either in early spring just as the new green blades are emerging or in late fall after growth has finished) and the clippings removed to keep fertility low. If left uncut, the blades will grow to 12 to 15 inches in length and will fall over to form a 6-inch-high, gently undulating surface. Neil Diboll at Prairie Nursery in Wisconsin developed some of the first fescue blends for low-care lawns, and still sells them under the name "No-Mow Lawn"; other nurseries sell their own blends under various names.

In the humid Mid-Atlantic and U.S. Southeast, lilyturf (*Liriope*) is a low-care, heat-tolerant option. Clump-forming *L. muscari* is easier to keep in check, while running *L. spicata* will quickly fill an area and can be managed by cutting it back at the edges. Both grow about 10 to 12 inches high in full sun to dense shade and are very drought-tolerant. They form spikes of flowers in summer, followed by black berries that can be sown to make more plants. Foliage persists through winter but may turn brown in colder zones. Lilyturf crowns (the base of each clump, where leaves emerge) can be damaged by mowing, but if you want to chop up last year's dead foliage, you could mow once at your mower's highest setting, in early spring before new growth begins.

Finer-bladed and lower-growing mondo grass (*Ophiopogon japonicus*) and dwarf mondo (*O. j.* 'Nanus') do well in shade or sun, but they need supplemental water while

Some years this northern mixed fescue lawn is not cut at all, and some years it is cut once after the seedheads have formed.

they are establishing and in dry periods thereafter. Unlike lilyturf, foliage stays green through the winter, and their flowers are small and inconspicuous. Mondo lawns also take longer to fill in and are on the expensive side, as they must be established using plants rather than seed. However, once established, they stay low (mondo is 6 inches high and dwarf mondo can be as low as 2 inches). If you purchase a few plants or get some from a gardening friend, you can separate them into tiny sprigs and plant them 6 inches apart on bare soil that has been improved with a 3-inch layer of compost. Give them a few years to spread to full coverage; during that few years, you'll need to weed between them. As with their larger relative lilyturf, mowing is not necessary for mondo and dwarf

*Dwarf mondo (*Ophiopogon japonicus *'Nanus') makes rounded, dark green tufts of foliage that gradually fill in to form a thick, nearly care-free evergreen lawn.*

mondo lawns. If you do want a very smooth, flat surface, make sure your lawnmower is set high enough that it won't damage the plants' crowns.

Several low, clump-forming sedges native to the U.S. Southeast are especially well adapted to hot, humid climates. Among them are reflexed sedge (*Carex retroflexa*), which prefers afternoon shade; sand sedge (*C. perdentata*), which can take sun or shade; and spreading sedge (*C. laxiculmis*, especially in its selection 'Hobbs'), which is best in shade with regular water. For high-traffic areas, the aggressive greenwhite sedge (*C. albolutescens*) is also low and clump-forming, but it fills in by heavily self-sowing and may spread to surrounding areas.

In the more arid regions of the West and Southwest, several native grasses can be used as single-species stands or in blends. Researchers at the Lady Bird Johnson Wildflower Center in Austin, Texas, have settled on a blend of buffalograss (*Bouteloua dactyloides*), blue grama (*B. gracilis*), and curly mesquite (*Hilaria belangeri*) as the best low-care lawn for these areas. These native grasses need little or no water; if you want them to stay green through dry periods, you will need to water them, but at a much lower rate than you would Kentucky bluegrass and other traditional turfgrasses. They prefer low fertility, too, so should not be fertilized, as that will encourage weeds over the grasses. (High-traffic lawns are an exception; they can benefit from an application of compost in the fall.) For best density, they should be cut no lower than 3 inches and should be allowed to form seeds to self-repair any gaps. After mowing, the clippings can be left on the lawn.

Many designers and gardeners in California swear by dune sedge (*Carex pansa*), a clump-forming, dark green native of the Pacific Coast region. It grows 6 inches high without mowing and can tolerate moderate foot traffic. It grows in full sun and is evergreen in mild climates. It will go dormant in dry conditions without regular water.

At universities across the country, researchers continue to test and develop species for lawns that will demand less irrigation and less frequent mowing. Botanical gardens, commercial growers, and gardeners are also trialing a variety of alternative lawn plants. You will get the best advice from reputable regional growers, who will be glad to provide instructions for establishing and maintaining lawns with the plants or seeds that they sell, and from local experts at a nearby university extension office or botanical garden.

all grown up

People who are sick of mowing often wonder, "What would happen if I just let my lawn grow?" The answer depends on several variables: the species in and the soil under your lawn, whether your lawn is in shade or sun, the potential weeds in your area, and your lawn maintenance strategies to date.

Some folks who let their lawns grow will initially see a mix of tall grasses, perhaps with an understory of short grasses or sedges, and perhaps dotted with speedwell, dandelion, hawkweed, wood sorrel, and other lawn "weeds" that finally get to bloom and form seedheads. Over time, this mix will evolve and better-adapted plants will outcompete the rest, probably leaving a less diverse area with various patches of competitive species. You may be able to maintain this managed meadow with once-a-year mowing to remove any woody plant seedlings that come in via birds, wind, or squirrels.

If you have meticulously kept your lawn as a grass-only area by regularly removing broadleaf plants, then letting it grow may result in a stand of pure grasses. Depending on the species, the site, and the surrounding plants, you may be able to mow much less often (for instance, when you host the annual neighborhood picnic) and simply think of it as a managed meadow that can become a lawn whenever you need one. If the species in your lawn

A tranquil garden offers a drought-tolerant lawn of blue grama (Bouteloua gracilis) *and a sunny bench.*

can cover the ground quickly and hold their territory against other plants, then you may be able to replace your regular herbicide applications with spot-treating or hand-weeding if you want to keep broadleaf plants out. And because you are letting the grasses keep their leaves, they won't need as much water to replenish them, so you can reduce or eliminate supplemental watering. Finally, if you let the grasses form seedheads, they will overseed themselves to keep your managed meadow thick and healthy, eliminating that chore as well.

On a hill under tall oaks where they rarely go, a Minnesota couple has let their turfgrass grow to its natural height. After two years, their managed meadow is mainly Kentucky bluegrass with scattered other turfgrass species. The blades of the grasses are 6 to 12 inches long or more, but they bend over to form a lower carpet that is easy to walk on. The seedheads are held above the foliage, but most are airy and inconspicuous. This managed meadow is cut once a year. Other maintenance includes

The homeowners have let a rarely used lawn "grow up" into a managed meadow. Keeping it cleared of tree seedlings requires much less effort than grooming it to traditional standards, and from a distance it still looks like a lawn.

occasional pulling of oak seedlings and weeds that arrive on the wind. The managed meadow looks no different from other lawns when viewed at a distance and has significantly cut the homeowners' weekly mowing time. They feel they've made a good trade.

"Kentucky bluegrass can be maintained as a no-mow area quite nicely," affirms Robert Mugaas, extension educator in horticulture and turfgrass management at the University of Minnesota. Though the area would not require mowing, he advises mowing once or twice a year to prevent excessive accumulation of clippings that can potentially smother the grasses. "It is best to mow when the grass is dry," he adds, "to more finely chop up the clippings and distribute them uniformly over the surface." If you leave the clippings on the grass, they will act as a slow-release fertilizer, providing the equivalent of about one fertilizer application annually.

Kentucky bluegrass requires a more fertile soil than the fine fescues and dry-adapted grasses mentioned earlier, so even if you leave your clippings after mowing, Robert recommends fertilizing a bluegrass-dominated area once in early fall with a pound of nitrogen per 1,000 square feet, to give it better color and vigor. No watering would be necessary except during prolonged periods of extreme heat and drought, because you are not regularly mowing.

freedom lawns

A great many little plants make their way into a lawn and persist despite periodic mowing. Instead of getting rid of the clover, chickweed, dock, creeping charlie, and other low-growing, broadleaf plants, why not just mow them too? Many plants other than grass can tolerate mowing and feel good to walk on. They may even be fragrant. Or they may perform services like pollination and pest control. Your freedom lawn could do more work, while you do less.

*Happy feet! Go barefoot without a care in a chemical-free lawn that allows broadleaf species, such as these white violets (*Viola*), to grow among the grasses.*

White clover (*Trifolium repens*) is a prime example of a broadleaf species that can be a beneficial addition to a lawn. It was a common component of lawn seed mixes back before broadleaf herbicides became a widely used lawn care strategy. Clover was valued as a built-in fertilizer for the grasses, through its ability to fix atmospheric nitrogen, and also for extending the lawn's season of green. Black medick (*Medicago lupulina*) and birdsfoot trefoil (*Lotus corniculatus*), other common lawn "weeds," are also nitrogen fixers, though they are considered invasive in some parts of North America.

White clover is not necessarily drought-tolerant (as Susan Harris discovered in her "lawn alternative testing ground"), so it may be that other broadleaf plants would better suit your freedom lawn. Nurseries are beginning to sell regionally blended grass and broadleaf "lawn" mixes that include clover, chamomile, English daisies, and

*It's spring, and the arboretum's five-year-old blue sedge (*Carex flacca*) lawn is just starting to green up.*

In summer, the finely fringed flowerspikes of blue sedge catch the light and flutter in the breeze.

similar low flowering plants. Or you can overseed your lawn with your own favorites.

Here are just a few of the long list of short plants you could include in a lawn that will be subject to moderate traffic: sweet alyssum (*Lobularia maritima*), several creeping speedwells (*Veronica*), creeping mazus (*M. miquelii*), Irish moss (*Sagina subulata*), Corsican mint (*Mentha requienii*), pennyroyal (*M. pulegium*), creeping jenny (*Lysimachia nummularia*), bugleweed (*Ajuga reptans*), Corsican sandwort (*Arenaria balearica*), creeping thyme (*Thymus serpyllum*), dwarf cupflower (*Nierembergia repens*), rock fleabane (*Erigeron scopulinus*), variegated pennywort (*Hydrocotyle sibthorpioides*), moss campion (*Silene acaulis*), brass buttons (*Leptinella squalida*), creeping cinquefoil (*Potentilla reptans*), golden oregano (*Origanum vulgare* 'Aureum'), baby's tears (*Soleirolia soleirolii*), alpine betony (*Stachys monieri*), many violets (*Viola*), many low sedums, many low pinks (*Dianthus*), English daisies

(*Bellis perennis*), and Roman chamomile (*Chamaemelum nobile*).

Not only does it cost more and take more time to use broadleaf herbicides on your lawn, but they can have adverse health effects for you, your children, your pets, and wildlife. You may want to learn more about these risks as you consider how important it is that your lawn be made entirely of grasses. It could be that you will decide to live with leaves of other shapes too.

Most American families with young children would prefer to have a lawn at home, especially in this modern age when "stranger danger" is a significant worry. Young children need to move their bodies, and a home lawn provides a safe, supervised area in which to run, crawl, and roll around. Consider that a freedom lawn, with its diversity of plants (minus any spiny plants that hurt to put a bare hand or foot on), may make a more interesting play area for your child. Children will appreciate the variety of leaves and flowers and the chance to play the games their parents played: making daisy chains, painting their chins gold with dandelions, and hunting for four-leaf clovers.

seasonal shifts

Along the walk near the main outdoor dining area at the Minnesota Landscape Arboretum, a slope is planted with blue sedge (*Carex flacca*), a grass-like plant with blue-green blades. Depending on the season, this unconventional lawn is 6 to 12 inches high. It's showier than traditional turf but needs much less care.

In spring, the newly greening mounds of this sedge dot the slope. In summer, the blue leaf blades stand erect and produce delicate flowerspikes. The male spikes form at the ends of blades; they are narrow, purple-brown pods with russet fringes. The female spikes arch out from the blades a few inches lower; they have dense clusters of round seeds and creamy yellow fringes. As summer passes, the female spikes remain visible, turning gray and twig-like as the blades fall over, making a shaggy carpet. The blades take on yellow highlights as the first frost approaches and are gradually packed down over the winter, when the lawn is generally hidden by snow.

This seasonally interesting alternative to turfgrass requires very little care and input from arboretum staff. For the first few years the slope wasn't cut at all, says Duane Otto, a landscape gardener at the arboretum, and now the plan is to mow once a year in early spring, to "tidy it up" and reveal the emerging leaves. Despite the bare soil between the mounds, the planting has not been troubled by weeds. Blue sedge is drought-tolerant and would need no supplemental watering, Duane says, but here in this public landscape it is watered during dry periods.

Blue sedge doesn't need full sun, and in fact, it grows best in part shade on soil that doesn't get waterlogged. In moister areas, it fills in with rhizomes to form a more uniform sod, but in a dry area like this, it retains visibly

Blue sedge offers dried seedheads in the fall.

separate clumps. Its deep roots hold the slope against erosion and capture runoff from rainstorms and snow-melt. Blue sedge is a subtly colorful, low-care ground-cover for places that won't have high traffic and that you don't want to mow or water, as well as for shadier areas where turfgrass struggles.

to water, or not to water

Native plant enthusiasts Roger Rosentreter and Ann DeBolt live on a long lot within the city limits of Boise, experimenting with dry-climate plants, particularly those that need little or no supplemental water. Ann is also a natural communities specialist for the Idaho Botanical Garden, helping to develop information and demonstration gardens showing area residents how to use less water and more regionally adapted plants in their landscapes.

Boise is classified as high desert: it receives 8 to 12 inches of precipitation a year, the majority of it during

the winter, and most typical garden plants, including turfgrasses, can only survive there with supplemental water. Ann and Roger have trialed several lawns made entirely of sheep fescue (*Festuca ovina*), a blue-tinted grass, slower growing than traditional turfgrass, that prefers dry climates. In places where they irrigate their sheep fescue lawn, it requires about half the water of standard turfgrass. Their irrigated sheep fescue lawn is cut three or four times per year at a 4-inch height, which keeps it low enough for walking but helps it to be more drought-tolerant than a shorter lawn. This lawn remains a serene blue-green throughout the growing season.

Another sheep fescue lawn that they don't irrigate at all survives this high desert climate by going dormant during the dry summer months. Its summer color is a warm, bright gold—very different from the cool blue-green of spring and fall. They have also created a low-maintenance bed of sheep fescue alongside a path. This bed is left unirrigated and is cut once a year in early summer to remove the seedstalks before the grass can self-sow, preserving its pattern of low, repeating mounds.

Sheep fescue grows well from seed, unlike some other drought-tolerant lawn plants such as mondo grass (*Ophiopogon japonicus*) and oak sedge (*Carex pensylvanica*), making a sheep fescue lawn more affordable to establish. It also tolerates light shade, and its low water need makes it a good, noncompetitive understory plant for some trees and shrubs. Even where it is irrigated enough to retain its color and soft texture through the growing season, a sheep fescue lawn will save water, money, and work, and as Roger and Ann's unirrigated bed demonstrates, this plant can also be a bold feature in a low-care xeric garden.

meadow meets lawn

In her small, sloping, suburban front yard, Karen Graham created a low and lawn-like woodland meadow by planting plugs of oak sedge (*Carex pensylvanica*) and a few

*top: An irrigated lawn of sheep fescue (*Festuca ovina*) uses about half the water of a traditional lawn, stays low with two to four mowings a year, and doesn't go dormant in the summer.*

bottom: An inventive display of unirrigated sheep fescue turns gold and dormant in midsummer, greening up again when cool weather comes.

seedlings each of wild ginger (*Asarum canadense*), wild geranium (*G. maculatum*), and early meadowrue (*Thalictrum dioicum*). Oak sedge naturally grows with oak trees, which abound throughout her neighborhood and the nearby county park. The other three plants typically grow with the sedge in woodlands and tolerate dry soil and shade. All are native to her region of the Upper Midwest.

Oak sedge can tolerate more shade than many grasses; it works well below taller grasses in a prairie planting and even under trees and shrubs. Its fresh green color is a desirable addition to most landscapes. It greens up early in the year, stays 6 to 8 inches high without mowing, spreads by rhizomes (giving more even coverage than a clump-forming grass), and has tiny seedheads that are interesting close-up but inconspicuous from a distance. Wild ginger keeps to shadier areas that are untouched by afternoon sun. Its unusual red-brown flowers, which are hidden under the leaves, "look like baby birds with their wide-open beaks begging for food," says Karen. Early meadowrue makes a winsome companion with its small rounded leaves that stand out against the lines of the sedge. In summer it grows 12 to 16 inches high and dangles tiny fringed white flowers above the other plants. Low, mounding wild geranium blooms nearly all summer, and its lacy velvet leaves look like green snowflakes.

After several years, other wild plants have moved into this meadow, including violets (*Viola*), Virginia waterleaf (*Hydrophyllum virginianum*), and jack-in-the-pulpit (*Arisaema triphyllum*). Animals have moved in too. Small birds will often hop around under the umbrellas of the wild ginger; perhaps they are feasting on the ants that collect its seeds. "The result has been delightful," says Karen, "and brings many compliments from neighbors and passersby."

The adjacent lawn has struggled, and because she gives the area no supplemental water or fertilizer, the better-adapted oak sedge is gradually overtaking it. She mows every spring to better see the emerging green blades

*A low meadow of oak sedge (*Carex pensylvanica*) and companions thrives on a dry suburban slope under maples and oaks.*

of the oak sedge, and she leaves the clippings on it as mulch.

This is an instance where doing less work has led to a lower-care and healthier landscape. Because Karen has preserved the harsh growing conditions, it is hard for typical weeds to get a foothold. Her low and low-care woodland meadow will dominate because it is well adapted to this dry shady site, but in more fertile, moister soil, it might not outcompete a lawn or blown-in weeds.

The oak sedge blooms in early spring. "They have sweet little flowers which look like a blue mist hovering over the grass," says Karen. "As I sit on my bench and look at the quiet beauty tucked into this wooded landscape, I am refreshed."

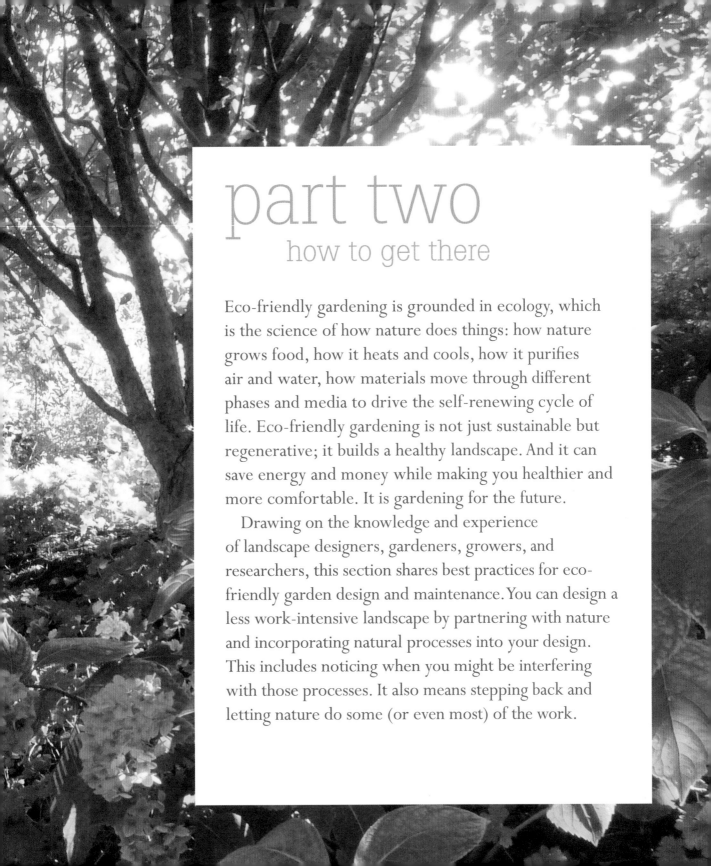

part two
how to get there

Eco-friendly gardening is grounded in ecology, which is the science of how nature does things: how nature grows food, how it heats and cools, how it purifies air and water, how materials move through different phases and media to drive the self-renewing cycle of life. Eco-friendly gardening is not just sustainable but regenerative; it builds a healthy landscape. And it can save energy and money while making you healthier and more comfortable. It is gardening for the future.

Drawing on the knowledge and experience of landscape designers, gardeners, growers, and researchers, this section shares best practices for eco-friendly garden design and maintenance. You can design a less work-intensive landscape by partnering with nature and incorporating natural processes into your design. This includes noticing when you might be interfering with those processes. It also means stepping back and letting nature do some (or even most) of the work.

converting your lawn to a garden

Removing your lawn is a one-time project, and spending time and effort to do it well will pay off. Your garden will spring to life more quickly if you get rid of the unwanted plants—all of them—before adding your desired plants. Unwanted plants take up water and nutrients when vulnerable new plants most need them.

smothering

One effective method of removing lawn is to smother it. That is, pile other materials on top of it, shutting off its supply of light and perhaps water too. You can use a variety of materials for smothering.

To convert your lawn to rich topsoil and give your garden a healthy start, smother your lawn using materials that will decompose. Mow it first at the shortest height of your mower to check its growth. You can leave the clippings, as they will add organic matter. Directly onto your mown lawn, place a layer of thick cardboard, or sheaves of newspaper, or old fabrics or carpets that are made from natural materials such as jute, wool, and cotton. Overlap the pieces, so that no light will penetrate to the ground. Top this biodegradable weed barrier with several inches of mulch, then wait for the lawn to die. It could take up to a year or longer to kill persistent plants like Canada thistle or bermudagrass, but if your lawn is made up primarily of cool-season turfgrasses, it should be dead within two to four months.

Shrink the lawn, plant a "habitat hedge," and you'll have something to look at from your lawn chair.

To plant immediately, you can dig through the layers of your smothered lawn to make holes in the soil below for your new plants. It works well to cut an X shape with your shovel and peel back the four pointed ends of your weed barrier. After you have planted, water your new plants well, then replace the weed barrier and mulch to keep your lawn from re-emerging; the planting process will go much faster if you use plugs instead of larger potted plants. Then you can just cut a slit through the weed barrier and slip them into the soil. If you have used a biodegradable weed barrier, you can establish new plants by seeding over the top of a smothered lawn; spread a couple of inches of good, seed-free soil directly on top of the weed barrier and sow seeds into it.

Black plastic makes an effective and convenient non-biodegradable weed barrier. However, it may not be the best choice for low maintenance or for your garden's long-term health. Plastic is impervious to water, so if you plant any plants through it, they will need supplemental water regardless of how much precipitation you receive; manually water directly into the planting holes or set up drip hoses before you lay down the plastic. Plastic will block water to any roots below it, so site your plastic weed barriers with nearby tree roots in mind. Rainwater will pool on the plastic in level areas (making prime mosquito habitat) and create runoff from sloped areas, so you will want to incorporate those factors into your design.

Unlike biodegradable materials, plastic does not contribute to building your garden's soil. Because it creates a "dry zone" by keeping water out, and because of the intense heat it generates, it may kill off beneficial soil organisms and disrupt or interrupt nutrient cycling. In contrast, biodegradable weed barriers will decompose, contributing nutrients and organic matter to make new soil, and while they are decomposing they will build up populations of beneficial soil microorganisms and fungi that will be in place, ready to support your new plants.

Plastic is energy-intensive to produce, and after use, it will wind up in a landfill or incinerator, whereas using a biodegradable weed barrier removes potential waste from the waste stream and converts it into soil and eventually into plants and animals, returning it to the cycle of life.

Landscape fabric looks like black plastic, but it is a layer of synthetic fabric with many small holes in it to let water through. Like plastic, it makes an effective and convenient weed barrier with some significant drawbacks. It is less prone to pool water or keep it from your plants, though it will slow the rate at which water can be absorbed into your landscape. Unlike a biodegradable weed barrier, it is a temporary solution and might create more work for you later; it will degrade (but not decompose) within a few years, so you will have shreds of it across your soil unless you pull it out while it is still intact. And like plastic, it takes energy to produce and becomes waste after a brief period of use.

To easily start a garden that you can plant in right away over an existing lawn, install raised beds made of wood or rock directly on top of a biodegradable weed barrier. Fill the beds with a deep layer of good soil, then plant. Mulch with a light layer of straw or sow seeds of quick-starting plants to hold the soil. Make paths between your beds using a weed barrier topped with chipped brush, gravel, or another slow-to-decompose material. This is an easy and effective design for a kitchen garden.

You can use smothering on a larger scale by building a berm or hill using soil, sand, or rock. If your berm is several feet deep, you won't need to lay down a weed barrier first. However, you will need to pack the berm; it may require heavy machinery to do this well. Packing is a crucial step, and even a well-packed berm will lose about a third of its height during its first few years as it is further consolidated by the slow processes of weather and gravity. Depending on the materials you use, you may need to add a layer of topsoil after packing. Minimize

*A sloped urban front lawn awaits transformation
under black plastic.*

erosion by using a thickly seeded living mulch or a thick
layer of mulch over the entire berm, spread around and
between your new plants. Mulch any paths as well.

tilling

If the soil under your lawn is not already light and fluffy,
and if it does not contain tree roots, it could be beneficial
to till before you put in your garden. This will loosen
your soil, creating air pockets to hold more water and
nutrients and to allow easier root penetration, so your
new plants can get established more quickly.

Tilling can be done manually with a variety of tools
from a hoe to a shovel to a pickaxe, or you can rent a
motorized rototiller. Note that tilling (even rototilling)
does not eliminate all the weeds or even all the grasses;
for best results, smother after tilling to kill off those
that remain. Optionally, you can water and wait for new
plants to sprout, then till again.

One big caution about tilling: it can spread and
multiply certain types of plants (like running thistles,
bermudagrass, and creeping charlie) that have the ability
to regenerate from small pieces of root or stem. If these
plants are growing in your lawn or landscape, you may
want to choose a different lawn removal method or be
sure to smother your lawn after it is tilled.

solarizing

Some landscapes, particularly old pastures and fields, are
home to well-established, persistent weeds that will not
easily be smothered by a biodegradable weed barrier or
eliminated by tilling. In these areas, you'll have better
luck solarizing with thick black plastic (3 mil or thicker),
purchased in rolls from a farm supply store. Mow the
area as short as you can first, then spread the plastic
across the ground and top it with a thin layer of mulch

to press it flat. Flattened this way, it can generate enough heat to kill weed seeds on the soil surface. Being impervious to water, it will block the ground from receiving water as well as light, which will be an additional blow to tougher plants.

You will need to solarize until the plants are dead; depending on the sun exposure, this may take only a week or two, or it could take several months to a year to effectively kill off persistent and deep-rooted plants. If you lay down plastic in the fall and leave it over the winter, often the area will be ready to plant during the next spring or summer. Once the area is killed, move the plastic to the next spot you wish to solarize. Thick plastic can be reused several times. It will last longer when it is protected from direct sunlight by a layer of mulch.

After you remove the plastic from a solarized area, you can top off the area with a couple of inches of fresh soil to give your new plants a head start and to prevent buried seeds from sprouting when the area receives water. Plant new plants or sow new seeds directly into this soil. You may also wish to add a layer of compost to replenish the soil life that was killed off by the extreme heat and dryness generated under the plastic.

Take care when using black plastic to solarize areas around trees and other established plants, as it won't let water through to their roots. Ways around this include solarizing only a third of the root zone at a time, and/or punching tiny holes in the plastic after it is laid, which will let some water drain down without letting plants grow up through it.

cutting away sod

You can cut away your lawn to establish a garden. Cut strips in your turf using a straight-edged spade or a sod-cutter, then roll up and remove the strips. Very few weeds will remain, though you will also have less topsoil.

Removing strips of lawn will be much easier if you first remove taprooted plants like dandelions, as their deep roots anchor the turf to the ground. Several easy-to-use tools are available for pulling up taprooted plants, including a simple fishtail-shaped tool that functions like a knife blade as well as a post-like tool you can use without stooping. Pulling taprooted plants can be as quick and effective as spot-treating them with poison, plus you will avoid harming your soil organisms.

Rather than removing your entire lawn, you can cut away the lawn where you want to make paths or patios, and pile the sod where you want to make planting beds. Removing the topsoil will give your paved areas a firmer base and decrease fertility, making those areas less attractive to weeds. Meanwhile, the extra topsoil and decomposed sod will form a deeper, richer soil in the planting beds.

Conversely, gardeners in arid landscapes can make a low-water design by cutting away the sod in future planting areas and piling it on future paths and patios, which should be sloped slightly to direct runoff into the adjacent planted areas. This easy earthshaping will send runoff right to the plants, for free and for the foreseeable future, without you ever giving it another thought.

poisoning

Scientific research continues to uncover negative health and environmental effects from our widespread use of lawn and garden chemicals. With all the other available options, it seems wise to limit our use of pesticides (which include herbicides, insecticides, and fungicides) in general and, where possible, to choose other ways to kill off areas of lawn.

It is important to understand the consequences of poisoning an area as you make your choice about how to remove your lawn. Using an herbicide kills not only the plants but also many soil microorganisms, so it will degrade your landscape, in contrast to the methods just discussed, which build soil even as they remove your lawn. Herbicides can also have negative effects on the surrounding landscape, including aquatic life in nearby lakes and streams.

However, it is also important to distinguish between poisoning an area once, in order to hasten its conversion from lawn to a lower-maintenance, more beautiful, or more useful landscape, and the routine use of chemical poisons to maintain your landscape. If your lawn is maintained using pesticides and synthetic fertilizers (which also have negative consequences for water quality and aquatic life), and a one-time dose of glyphosate would kill it and allow you to establish a garden that won't need regular doses of chemicals to stay healthy, that will be a significant positive change in the long term.

If you do poison your lawn, you can leave the dead lawn in place and plant new plants directly into it. You can also add a couple of inches of new soil on top of the dead lawn, sow seeds, and top with a light layer of straw.

Some gardeners turn to herbicides as the best option for removing sloped lawns, but even on a steep slope, you have other options. You can smother or solarize a slope using rocks or bricks to hold down your weed barrier, or you can till a slope; just be prepared to seed or plant it right away, and after seeding but before planting, tack down woven straw mats (available from landscape supply stores) to hold the loose material in place while your new plants are emerging. You can plant through these mats, and they will work better than mulch to protect soil and seeds from sliding downhill.

mulching

Mulch can be made from a variety of materials. Chipped brush (wood chips) from trimmed trees and shrubs may be available from your city or county, or from a local tree trimmer or power company. The quality and composition of chipped brush varies widely, depending on the season of the year and on the equipment used. In summer it will contain leaves, making it quicker to decompose and a better short-term weed deterrent and nutrient source for your plants. Chipped brush from either end of the growing season that doesn't contain leaves can make good path material; it is slower to decompose and less attractive to weeds.

Living mulches—plants that thickly cover bare ground—are used to prevent erosion and keep unwanted plants from moving in. A living mulch can be established by seed and other plants planted through it later. It can also be seeded around existing plants. Choose a living mulch that will be a good companion to your other plants; consider its growth habit in relation to theirs, and whether it generally improves the soil or strongly competes for water and nutrients. A living mulch can be used to hold bare ground temporarily, then tilled or smothered to make way for your permanent plants. A walkable living mulch can be used as a path surface.

A bale of straw (not hay, which includes seeds) makes an inexpensive and beneficial mulch. It is especially good for vegetables and is easy to remove with a rake when it's time to plant the next crop. It is fluffy, so it contains a lot of air that will trap heat, keeping the soil warm and helping your seedlings grow faster. A layer of straw efficiently preserves soil moisture and can drastically reduce the amount of supplemental water your plants need from you. As straw decomposes, it makes a slow-acting fertilizer for plants or a nitrogen-rich material to add to the compost pile.

Crushed rock and gravel may make effective mulches in dry climates as they can hold moisture at the soil surface and even condense moisture out of the air. They are better mulches than wood chips for plants that need excellent drainage. In wetter areas, gravel makes a good seed bed and therefore a poor mulch. To keep gravel looking fresh, it will need to be raked periodically and have leaves removed.

You may have access to other local, natural materials that could be useful as mulch. Your municipality might process collected yard waste into mulch and compost and offer them free to residents. Local industrial waste products will be plentiful and inexpensive or free: ground up shells near the coast, spent hops near a brewery, and other possibilities for smothering abound.

One word of caution: check that there are no toxic components in the material you plan to use before you bring it into your garden. For instance, while chipped brush won't normally contain chemicals, chipped wood from construction sites and other sources may include wood treated with arsenic or other heavy metals. These contaminants can leach out of the wood into your soil, and from there into your food plants. Be sure to use only materials that will not be hazardous to your family's health or your garden's health.

planting and seeding

After removing your lawn, you may choose to plant or seed your new garden area. Different methods are effective in different regions and sites, but here are some general considerations.

Some seeds grow easily whatever the conditions, and you won't need to do more than just scatter them on the ground to get them to grow. For more finicky seeds, make sure the ground is loosened and provides a relatively flat surface by raking it with a short-tined metal rake. Scatter the seed, then cover with a fine layer of soil if necessary. Most seeds come with instructions. Depending on what you are planting, you can pat down, pack down, or roll over the planted seeds with a seed roller. Sprinkle with a light haze of water to avoid displacing the seeds. Covering them with a thin layer of straw will hold in moisture and protect against bird predation and wind

as the seeds are germinating, while still letting in some light. Keep them moist while they germinate—you may have to water daily or more often—and then back off on watering as the seedlings emerge.

If you are planting plants, you can choose from very small sizes called plugs, or tiny to large pots. Smaller plants can get established more quickly, but until they do, they are more fragile. Take care to do as little damage as possible to their roots when planting. Larger potted plants can sustain more root and leaf damage as they have more of each. If their roots are pot-bound, you can break apart the rootball or even cut it with a knife to encourage new roots to move into the surrounding soil more quickly.

You will get different advice about how to dig a hole depending on whom you consult. Advice varies from making it twice as wide as the branch spread to cutting a deep slit and sliding the roots into it. The shape and size of the hole will matter less if your soil is light and airy than if it is compacted. You might try filling your hole with water if you can—some soils will be too well drained for this—then adding the plant and replacing the soil you dug out, making a big mud pie.

It may be tempting to fertilize a plant really well at the time of transplanting, to give it a boost of nutrition to make up for the shock. Most experts now discourage this as it may stress the plant. Some plants grow best without any soil amendments, and for the others, adding compost in the planting hole or as a light mulch after planting is a gentler way to ensure that nutrients are available as the plant needs them.

When the plant is in the hole and the soil has been replaced, thoroughly water it and gently tamp down the wet soil over its roots. Tamping too firmly can press the air and water out of the soil around the plant, so do it just firmly enough that the roots come into good contact with the soil.

Vegetable seedlings in a wooden box, ready to be planted.

irrigating

Irrigating less or not at all is one of the benefits of trading in your traditional turfgrass. As you transform your yard into an eco-friendly garden, you can redesign it to use water more wisely. As far as possible, design your garden to succeed given your climate's natural water supply. Try to restrict any irrigation to high-use and high-impact areas.

If you are starting from scratch, you can reduce or eliminate your need for irrigation by shaping your landscape to catch and hold the water that runs through it, whether it comes off your roof and driveway or down from the hills above your property. Berms, swales, and basins are time-tested earthshaping techniques that may take skill and labor to design but could free you from water worries for the life of your garden.

Another way to lower your water bill and design away work is to choose plants that are well adapted to your climate and site and will thrive with no supplemental water. These include your regional native plants, as well as plants from similar sites and climates. Note that all new transplants, especially larger trees and shrubs (even those that are native), may need supplemental irrigation until they have settled into their new home. Some gardeners continue to irrigate their native plants to prolong bloom or prevent dormancy, but even then, the well-adapted plants will need less water than those that prefer a wetter climate.

To design for the most efficient irrigation, put plants with similar water needs together. No irrigation will be needed in areas with well-adapted plants, and you can plan for different levels of irrigation in other areas. A shaded location, for instance, may need only occasional water during periods of drought, whereas a regularly watered zone might include a vegetable garden, container plants, annual bedding plants, and any remaining turf.

A smart irrigation system that is adjusted as the seasons change can efficiently handle this chore for you. Irrigation systems have come a long way since the days when sprinklers sprayed water across farm fields and extensive lawns during the heat of the day, with much of the water evaporating before it reached the ground.

Sprinkler systems use less water, because more of it gets to your plants, if the spray heads are aimed low and operate when the sun is down. You can make your sprinkler system more effective by replacing traditional spray heads with matched precipitation, low application rate heads that give your plants water slowly enough that they can use it all.

Soaker hoses and their upscale cousin, drip irrigation, are the most water-thrifty systems, delivering water directly to the root zone where it is needed, with little or no evaporation. They are the best choices for irrigating on sloping ground, as their slow flow rate reduces water wasted through runoff. They also maintain a healthy air/water balance in the soil, promoting optimal plant growth.

Garden centers sell soaker hoses that are the same diameter as a standard garden hose but are perforated all along their length. Lay soaker hoses directly on tilled or solarized ground, and below any weed barriers or mulch, to ensure that water will be delivered to your plants' root zones. Mulch over the top of soaker hoses to reduce evaporation, which can be a significant portion of water use, especially in dry climates.

Drip systems include an ever-expanding variety of lines, emitters, and other parts that can be connected as desired to bring water to your plants and bypass areas where you don't want to irrigate. Drip systems give you the ability to precisely control how much water gets to each area of your landscape. This makes it easy to establish different water use zones.

Whether you use sprinklers, hoses, or drip lines, don't waste water with a "set it and forget it" system. Invest in a smart controller that uses environmental sensors to decide how long and how frequently your plants get water. Make sure to adjust your irrigation schedule seasonally; your landscape's water needs change through the seasons, and so should the amount of water it gets from you. These strategies will cut your water use even further, and you'll have healthier, stronger plants with deeper root systems.

aftercare

Like any babies, new plants or seedlings will require more attention at first. If they get enough water and nutrients in early stages, they will grow out of their fragility faster. As that means less work for you later on, it is in your best interest to give them the help they need early on.

A layer of mulch can keep down weeds and conserve soil moisture. Compost can feed your plants and also boost microbial activity and diversity in your soil. For seeded areas you generally want the ground to stay moist until your seeds sprout. For newly transplanted plants, you want the soil to dry out between waterings but not to stay dry for any length of time.

Just observe and do your best to understand what your new plants are lacking and if they need you to supply it. Soon enough, if you've sited them well and they are comfortable in their new location, they will put out new growth, a sign that their roots are supplying them with adequate food and water. Then you can back off on your help.

implementing in phases

Divide your lawn-to-garden renovation into clear steps that you can take gradually over time, as your budget and energy allow. Begin with the area or element you most desire. Or the one that will solve the worst problem for you. Or the one you can actually finish. Or the one you can afford. You may want to plant young trees or espaliers first, or you may want to start with the area just outside your door because it will be appreciated and used most often.

Some gardens take relatively little time to set up—a berm can be built and seeded in one or two weekends—but other areas or living features will take many years to mature. For instance, a woodland garden may require a period of smothering the lawn, then planting trees and shrubs, then waiting until they have grown to cast enough shade before adding your ground-layer plants; or, alternatively, planting sun-loving ground-layer plants right away, then replacing them with shade-tolerant plants as the trees grow. During an area's transition, try to keep the ground covered at all times to prevent erosion and build up healthy populations of soil microorganisms. If you have tilled or otherwise created bare soil that you won't be planting right away, cover it with mulch or living mulch.

If you chafe at the length of the garden-building process, keep reminding yourself that you will get a better garden by taking the time to create hospitable conditions and nurture new plants. Just as childhood nutrition puts a person on the path to a lifetime of better health, nutrient-rich and well-structured soil will support your garden's long-term health. And unlike an unchanging lawn, your thriving, diverse, eco-friendly garden will get better every year. Your plants will grow, your soil will improve, communities above and below ground will increase their complexity and interconnections. As some garden areas mature, they will give more interest and satisfaction, which may make it easier to be patient with newer areas.

designing an eco-friendly garden

an eco-friendly garden that is well designed can be more self-sustaining, meaning less work and more pleasure for you over the years. Don't rush into making (or hiring someone else to make) a cookie-cutter garden ill suited to your landscape and lifestyle. Each design choice should be based not only on your aesthetics or comfort but also on the natural processes and character of your site.

envision

To design a garden, people will often gaze at the existing lawn (or bare dirt, after recent construction) and try to imagine where they should put the plants. For another approach, try imagining where you want to be walking, riding, or otherwise moving through your landscape...that's where you can put the paths. And where you need open areas to pursue your outdoor activities—playing volleyball, reading a book, sunbathing or swimming, growing food or eating it...those places will be your garden "rooms." All the space around those paths and rooms can be alive with plants and animals.

Notice the size of your garden's open areas; the larger they are, the more species of animal will not cross them. How will your tree frogs get from one grove to another? Connect the groves with unmowed corridors so you can hear their sweet singing (and glimpse their jewel-green faces) throughout your garden.

A patch of pollinator-attracting perennials and a birdfeeder ensure that wildlife often enlivens the view from inside this house.

Imagine what you want to see when you look out your windows. Those views are part of your environment during all the hours you spend indoors, in every season. Would you rather see a barren brown stretch (or white, if there is snow) all winter, or branches heavy with bright red berries and birds eating them? A great way to savor the changing seasons is to plant fruiting trees and shrubs outside your windows. Then, rather than parked cars or neighboring houses, you will see flowers in spring, foliage in summer, droplets along a branch when it's raining, and birds and berries in winter.

Further from your house, in places you don't visit or see as often, the most eco-friendly approach is to let go and let them be wilder. This can reduce your work and worry while letting more plants and animals share your land. Along with demanding less from you, wilder places can give you more: more opportunities to explore, more wildlife to watch, more chances to escape for a quiet walk alone with nature.

define

It makes sense to at least minimally define some areas of your garden. Barriers that contain and segregate spreading plants will lighten your workload. Physical cues that delineate paths will protect healthy, living soil from foot traffic and give people an easy journey through your landscape.

Edges can be ornamental as well as functional. Borders of rock or brick, short retaining or sitting walls, wattle, hedges, fences, and even water channels can be employed to divide garden spaces. The edges can be clear and abrupt, to give garden areas shape and definition, or they can be made wider, perhaps even allowed to merge, for more gradual transitions.

Whenever possible, choose gradual transitions over abrupt edges. For instance, if you want local turtles to be able to cross your garden, don't edge your path with a low wall. Turtles are often trapped on roads: they can get down the curb into the street, and defy death to cross it, but then they can't climb up the curb on the other side. Toads and other small garden residents may also be unable to climb over a barrier. Consider using ground-level transitions, like groundcovers or different kinds of paving, rather than taller barriers between garden areas. Or use willow hoops or fencing that is open at the bottom.

If one of your garden areas has a lawn or other running groundcover, your frequent attention may be needed to contain it unless you use a robust edge such as pavement or a dense border of plants with thick ground-level foliage. In the past, experts have recommended that a transitional strip of lawn be used between a walkway and a taller planted area, to increase visual appeal and signal that the planting is a garden rather than an "abandoned" landscape. This is generally a high-maintenance design. Lawn grasses may creep or self-sow into the adjacent planting. Tall plants may shade out the lawn or arch over it, making it harder to mow. The two areas may look jarring side by side, diminishing the visual power of your garden, especially if that garden is designed to evoke wild nature.

Where you want a low, open area next to pavement, a low groundcover could stay beautiful with less care than a lawn, and you could choose a groundcover that harmonizes better with your garden. A well-suited groundcover will need less or no mowing, watering, and fertilizing, and perhaps very little weeding once established. You could let it creep into the garden as an understory, tying the two areas together visually, or you could use a robust barrier to keep it separate from the garden; either strategy would design away work.

If the path or road is wide enough that you don't need a low area next to it, why not let your garden grow clear up to the pavement? This gives people who are walking past a richer sensory experience, letting them be briefly immersed in your garden.

A double edging of paved path and dense groundcover (Stachys byzantina 'Silver Carpet') effectively separates lawn from planting beds.

Mat-forming pussytoes (Antennaria neglecta) merges into these stepping stones and serves as an understory for the adjacent prairie planting, giving the garden a mature feel and decreasing edge-related maintenance.

populate

For an eco-friendly garden, it makes sense to prefer plants that are native to your region. In an arid climate, these plants will have growth, bloom, and fruiting cycles that are adapted to regional precipitation patterns. In a cold climate, the plants will know when to go dormant and when to emerge after winter. Non-native plants suited to your site and climate can also play key roles in creating a diverse and healthy living community, for instance, by extending the flowering season to support pollinators. You'll save work if you choose plants that will be able to grow to their full size and natural shape, rather than those that you must frequently prune, clip, or divide to keep them from obscuring a window or a path, or from overrunning their neighbors.

Many gardeners fall in love with new plants and start out by planting one of these and one of those…and one of pretty much any plant they can get their hands on. Unless you are an expert, with intimate knowledge of your site and the plants, some of your choices will fail. The best thing you can do is to learn from this how to make better choices. Try to figure out what led to each failure. Try to add more of the plants that succeed, or try plants that like similar conditions.

It may go against your grain to spread the plants that are thriving. They may seem too common or you may worry they will take over and make the garden look too boring. Really, the opposite is true. A site with characteristic plants will have a stronger personality than one with a bit of this and a bit of that. Those signature plants—the ones that are abundant and happy in your garden—help make it a recognizable, unique place.

So embrace your garden's emerging individuality, capitalize on its strengths, and multiply those signature plants. Think to yourself, "This worked here, so I'll try some more there" rather than always thinking, "I already have one of those, so I want something different." You can provide diverse companions for your signature plants—diversity is desirable for many reasons—but if a large number of your garden's plants are healthy and obviously thriving, it will look better to you and to everyone else too.

Planting in vertical layers—from tall trees down to lower trees, shrubs of all heights, and finally herbaceous ground-layer plants—creates a natural community of plants that can support each other's health, hold their territory against unwanted plants, and provide habitat for birds and wildlife. If you don't have trees or shrubs in your garden, you can still vertically layer your herbaceous plants to cover the ground and keep out weeds. Just keep adding shorter plants to fill in among and below the taller ones. Pay attention to a plant's growth habit when choosing its companions. In a low-water garden, you may want to retain bare ground between the plants to help your garden be more drought-tolerant, and in a wetter garden, you can keep weeds out more effectively by covering bare ground with your chosen plants.

connect

A healthy living community makes a resilient, low-care landscape. Plants and animals will form partnerships that help them to cycle water and nutrients, reusing waste products and converting them to new life in a continuous cycle. Your role in such a garden leans more toward enjoying and exploring these connections rather than keeping the landscape healthy. The garden is less dependent on you, and you are freer to enjoy it.

One easy way to make your garden more self-sustaining is to supply healthy companions for your trees. If a tree is grown in a traditional mown turfgrass lawn, chances are that neither plant is happy. Shade and root competition from trees stress most turfgrasses, and most trees want to be growing in a layer of leaf litter and decaying wood that is supporting fungi with whom they

Layered plant community at Olbrich Botanical Gardens,
*Madison, Wisconsin: under a row of cornelian cherries (*Cornus
mas *'Golden Glory'), occasional hydrangeas (*H. macrophylla
'Blushing Bride') are set in a groundcover of Geranium ×canta-
brigiense *'Biokovo'.*

have forged beneficial partnerships, in soil that has plenty of decomposers to recycle the wood and leaves into fresh nutrients that feed the tree.

Fungi—the underground organisms that produce the aboveground fruit we know as mushrooms—are valuable decomposers that turn dead wood, insect armor, and other hard-to-digest materials into tree food. While doing this important job, fungi develop elaborate networks in the soil, connecting with plant roots and interacting with soil organisms. Some fungi channel extra food and water to your tree. Some produce medicinal compounds that protect your tree from various disease microorganisms. The trees send carbohydrates through their roots that feed their connected fungi.

Compacted soil damages this web of connections (known as the soil food web) and makes it harder for soil organisms to find and link with each other. Synthetic fertilizers and pesticides kill soil organisms or cause them to flee, destroying the soil food web. Mowing a lawn and applying chemicals therefore creates a less hospitable environment for your trees.

Rather than lawn, grow ground-layer plants under your trees. This will protect the trees and their root zones from damage by weed whips, soil compaction, and desiccation, and it will create the kind of soil community that supports a healthy tree.

Ground-layer plants (including low and slow lawns) that aren't regularly cut develop deeper, spongier root masses. As their roots delve into the soil, they loosen it, creating pockets to hold water and nutrients and channels for soil creatures to move through. Ground-layer plants can shade the ground, keeping the root zone cooler and moister. They may drop foliage, which along with the tree's fallen foliage builds up into a protective layer of organic matter. This layer, called duff, holds the soil against erosion and encourages soil organisms to move up to the surface and begin their work of decomposing the duff. The soil organisms aerate the soil as they move around.

Adult birds may eat seeds, berries, or nectar, but they need protein-rich insects to feed their hatchlings.

The tree contributes by dropping its leaves, which add to the duff, and by attracting birds that perch in it and poop out nutrients, which add to the duff, and by hosting leaf- and wood-eating insects that live and die in or under the tree. Eventually they too give their bodies to the duff. This diverse duff created by living creatures above and below ground makes rich, nutritious soil, which grows a healthier garden.

When all these elements—tree, flying creatures, ground-layer plants, duff, and soil organisms—are present, they work together in complementary ways to create a living community that supports every one of them. If you take away one element of the community (for instance, by replacing ground-layer plants with mown turfgrass, or by raking away the leaves), you disrupt the connections that keep nutrients cycling through the community. Then you may have to step in and add water, or add fertilizer, or aerate the soil, or add soil to offset erosion, or control the populations of different organisms. If, on the other hand, you restore or retain all these parts of a living community, they will form connections with each other and do these jobs together, and you will not have to.

enliven

When you are ensuring that your garden has all the necessary parts of a healthy, living community, don't leave out the animals. They are crucial to keep the nutrients and water cycling through the landscape, and they will multiply the entertainment value and appeal of your garden too.

Animals add life to a landscape. We humans are curious about other animals and like to watch, learn about, and interact with them. Yet when we build the places we live, work, and play, we don't plan for sharing them with other animals. Most wild animals are not welcome in our private and public landscapes, our cities, our farms, our golf courses, our roadsides…all of which adds up to a lot of land from which wild animals are excluded.

More and more of the world's land is devoted to people's exclusive use, and researchers predict widespread extinctions of many species if we continue to take over land and exclude other animals. However, scientific studies also show that our choices as individual property owners can make a real difference, not just for individual animals, but in how many species survive extinction. While vast tracts of wildlife habitat are essential for long-term preservation and for biodiversity, small islands (such as your yard and mine) can be crucial for local populations and as migration corridors.

If you want to see animals living on your property rather than just stopping by for a visit, you must provide everything that a certain animal needs in order to eat, rest, mate, nest, and raise young there. These elements include cover, water, food, and nest-making materials.

Insects are a critical part of a healthy natural community. They are essential food for baby birds as well as adult birds, toads, bats, and other animals that are higher up in the food chain. They provide important services like pollination that keep plants surviving and reproducing. Some are critical for decomposing organic matter and converting it into nutrients. Overwintering insects in stems and leaves, including fallen leaves, are key protein sources for birds and other animals that remain in the area through the winter. If there are no insects in your yard, there will be a lot less life there.

Including regionally native plants in your garden will help it to support birds, butterflies, and other insect-eaters. Most leaf-eating insects are specialists, living on one species of plant that they have evolved to digest. Native plants also serve as larval food for butterflies; in their caterpillar stage, butterflies eat leaves, and most butterfly species use only one family of plants as a larval food.

Many of us have been brought up to abhor any insect, and to view them as unwanted pests that we should kill whenever we notice them. Rather than using traps or poisons that kill insects indiscriminately, consider methods that target a specific pest or protect individual plants (or people).

As for cover and nesting sites, shrubs are ideal. Most songbirds want to nest 4 to 10 feet above the ground in moderately dense to dense foliage. Berry-producing shrubs are bird magnets; they attract pollinators with their flowers and provide food in the form of berries, as well as giving nesting sites. Native berry-bearing shrubs do all that and more, attracting leaf-eating insects too, so they make ideal bird nurseries.

Shrubs provide a show for the gardener as well, with their vertical structures, foliage that may change color in fall, and masses of flowers and berries that make a bolder statement than shorter perennials. They also contribute to the garden year-round. Well-sited shrubs will need no pruning and can be left to grow to their natural shape and size. If you don't have the space to plant shrubs, a thick vine trained up an arch or wall can give you bird habitat.

For ground-based animals, shelter can be a simple pile of branches or a boulder. Mulch piles and rotting logs make warm, soft winter dens, and toads and lizards will burrow deep into them and hibernate. Many insects overwinter or leave the next generation's eggs in fallen leaves, so letting them stay in your garden will keep biodiversity high.

Water is another element that will persuade creatures to live in your yard rather than just passing through. Bird baths are useful for flying and climbing wildlife, but other animals need ground-level water. Make it accessible with a shallow beach or sloped banks.

Animals use a great variety of natural materials to build their nests, and the more diverse your available materials, the better your chances of hosting diverse animals. Hummingbirds camouflage their nests with an outer coating of lichens. The fluff of milkweed (*Asclepias*) and thimbleweed (*Anemone cylindrica*) is used by chickadees and goldfinches. Swallows employ mud. Magpies build elaborate nests with sticks. Nightingales use moss in the interior and oak leaves around the outside. Many birds bind their nests together with spiderwebs or dried grasses.

One last thing to note about animals is that they spend their lives at different vertical levels of the landscape. Different species prefer to perch and nest at different heights, so include branches and dense foliage at many heights in your garden. Animals may use more vertical layers if they are accessible. A fallen branch can connect the tree canopy with the ground in the same way that a wheelchair ramp allows access between a building and the street. A log that is partly submerged in a pond adds a whole dimension of possible activities for turtles, waterbirds, and other aquatic life...from basking to surveying the water's surface for insects to eating a crayfish in relative safety. A sloped bank or fallen tree allows more creatures to move between water and dry land. These bridges connecting the vertical layers of your landscape will improve its capacity to support more diverse life.

Aside from benefiting animals by increasing their habitat, there is another reason to design a wildlife-friendly garden, and that is for your own benefit. The natural world is not always the most comfortable place for people to spend time, and not the easiest to get to either. Most of us live in urban areas where we are increasingly cut off from the natural world in our daily lives. Your yard may be your best chance to experience nature daily. So when you are designing your garden, make it a place that will entice you away from that comfortable indoors, and one that will encourage you to form your own strong web of connections to the other species that share the world with us.

*Found treasure: a mossy
chickadee nest.*

maintaining
your garden

S ome people say that lawn is easier to maintain than any other type of landscape. Other people say lawn is more work and more expensive to maintain than anything else. Who is right? It's complicated.

Traditional turfgrass may demand frequent watering and cutting, as well as periodic aeration and fertilization. Low and slow lawn species, freedom lawns, and living carpets need less or none of those interventions, but they may require some weeding. So it is only true that lawns need more frequent maintenance than most other landscapes if we're talking about a perfect monoculture of thirsty turfgrass that is required to stay lush and green and short all year. Compared to that perfect lawn, the aforementioned low-care alternatives will certainly require less frequent work and attention from the gardener. So will many other types of landscapes, but it will be different work.

Lawn care is familiar to many of us—some of us have done it all our lives—but we may have no clue about how to care for other types of landscape. It is always harder to do something new than to repeat what you've done a zillion times before. But as you continue to repeat that unfamiliar chore, it gets easier.

What kinds of chores are we talking about? Periodically pruning woody plants. Periodically sweeping or raking pavement, gravel, and other open areas. Weeding. How often you do these things will depend on three things: your site, your design, and your standards. You don't necessarily have much control over your site, but in cases where change is possible, you may have to spend some money to make those changes. You have a lot of control over your design if you're starting fresh, but if you need to change existing features, that may cost you in money and time. As for your standards, changing them is free, though it could be painful.

A chipmunk helps the gardener by eating the copious maple seeds that fall in the garden every spring. Not only is this enjoyable to watch, but it means fewer maple seedlings to pull.

partnering with nature

What natural processes are at work in your site? Instead of fighting a (perhaps neverending) battle against those processes, can you think of a way to make them work for you? For example, if a certain plant is reproducing in your garden, it is a healthy and happy plant and may be a good candidate for one of your signature plants. Rather than being alarmed by its success, you could see it as a resource. This is not to say that you should let all seedlings grow up in your garden, as certain plants will kill off their fellows if you don't intervene. But many plants will reproduce when they are well sited, and that gives you a chance to inexpensively increase your garden with plants you know will succeed. Think of your extra plants as garden currency. A thriving garden will reward you with a supply of seedlings to share with your friends and fellow gardeners.

There are endless ways to turn extra materials generated by your garden into resources. Your ornamental grasses need to be cut every year; what if you dispose of or compost the seedheads, but use the remaining stems as straw to mulch your vegetable garden? Pine needles, fallen leaves, lawn clippings, and plant shearings can also become weed-deterring, gently fertilizing mulches. Use trimmed branches to train vines, build fences, or make brush piles for wildlife.

Another part of having a low-maintenance garden is to consciously choose to relax in your garden, rather than looking around and seeing unfinished work. Set a different standard of cleanliness for your outdoor rooms. Recognize that insects, mushrooms, and debris play important roles in a healthy and self-sustaining garden. Shed some of your responsibility and let a natural area look more natural. Chances are that it will function better, too, without so much "help" from you. Gardening in this way, you may not get the exact garden you had imagined. Instead you may be surprised and relieved to find you have a garden you can enjoy spending time in, one that will engage your interest and will evolve into a thriving natural community that includes you but does not depend on you. At least, not so much.

doing less

It's true: to have a more eco-friendly garden, you will probably need to stop doing so much work out there. Some traditional or commonly accepted gardening practices will actually undermine the health of a living community. Change these practices, keep or restore the necessary pieces, and you will see your garden rebuild its soil food web and become dramatically more self-sustaining.

Hold off on cutting down dead stalks until spring. The seeds and larvae in them are important food for overwintering birds, and they might be harboring your garden's next generation of insect predators. Enjoy these elements for their winter interest, and rather than seeing them as debris to be removed, learn to see them as nature's handy food storage containers.

Instead of removing dead branches, logs, or stumps, incorporate them into your garden. Dead wood is a rich food source for your landscape. Not only does it provide the raw materials that fungi and beetles convert into nutritious soil, but chickadees and other birds will nest in stumps, and woodpeckers will visit to eat the wood-boring insects in the dying wood. Make a brush pile (away from the house) to add habitat for small reptiles and rodents, then get ready to marvel at the visiting falcons.

Instead of mowing lawns and paths, design low, open areas and paths that won't ever need to be cut. Mowing impedes the movements of animals across your landscape.

Don't remove fallen leaves from your garden. Treat them as the valuable resource that they are, and use them to return nutrients to your soil, protect it from erosion, keep weeds at bay, preserve soil moisture, and boost soil life. If you don't have many leaves, you can usually leave

*If these milkweed (*Asclepias syriaca*) stalks are left standing over the winter, the fluff may be used for bird nests in the spring.*

them where they have fallen. Run the mower over light layers of fallen leaves on the lawn, and leave them as a mild natural compost. This can help your lawn green up in the spring, and it adds calcium, which can reduce dandelion populations in the lawn.

A light layer of leaves will pose no impediment to taller ground-layer plants and will gradually break down, adding nutrients to the soil. However, plants that need well-drained soil, such as low sedums or pinks (*Dianthus*), may suffer from fungal disease if a leaf layer keeps the soil around them too moist, and many mat-forming plants including mosses will die out if they are covered too long.

You can rake a deeper layer of excess leaves into planting beds under taller perennials, shrubs, or woodland natives that are adapted to emerging through a layer of duff every spring. One strategy to lessen your leaf-related workload is to make islands around your lawn trees, creating planting beds into which you can rake some of the fallen leaves. You might also add shrub islands in your lawn, giving you more places to put the leaves and increasing your garden's songbird habitat and four-season appeal.

Some types of leaves (like oak and evergreen magnolia) are tough or waxy and take longer to decompose. They may pack down and make it difficult for water to penetrate to the soil, and they may catch water and create mosquito habitat. If you can shred these leaves with your mower or a light-duty shredder, the resulting smaller volume of leaf mulch will break down more quickly and you may be able to use it throughout your garden.

In cases where your leaf layer is too deep for your plants, other strategies to try include piling the extras until they break down (like cold compost), adding them to your compost pile, or shredding them and using the resulting leaf mulch in your garden. You could also try designing away some or all of this work, for instance by replacing the plants under your trees with sturdy shrubs and bold perennials that can handle larger quantities of leaf litter.

Finally, even if you relied on poisons to get your garden started, remember that routine use of poisons to maintain your landscape simply isn't eco-friendly. Chemical fertilizers create unhealthy soil conditions that spur you to use more fertilizers and damage the soil food web. In place of synthetic fertilizers, help to restore the natural cycling of nutrients in your landscape by recognizing the valuable inputs of fallen leaves, nitrogen fixers, and other natural fertilizers and by nurturing a healthy soil food web. In areas with low fertility, well-adapted plants can outcompete most traditional weeds, and they can be used to create an eco-friendly landscape that demands less work from you.

Research continues to document the health risks of pesticides for you, your children, your pets, and other living creatures large and small. Instead of poisoning plants, investigate other weed removal methods and consider tolerating more diversity, particularly in your lawn. Instead of poisoning fungi, celebrate their presence as indicators of healthy soil life. Instead of poisoning insects, we must tolerate them in our landscapes if we want to see any other life there. Manage your insect populations by increasing the diversity of your plants, by bringing in more plants that attract insect predators, and by creating habitat for all insect eaters, from spiders, bats, and reptiles to baby birds and their parents.

making an eco-friendly lawn

If you are set on keeping some lawn, the starting point is obvious: shrink your lawn down to the size you actually use. Then you will be maintaining only the lawn that you need. Convert or restore the rest of your property to a more fulfilling, more functional, and less needy landscape. For areas you might shrink, look to steep, wet, far-away, and other less traffic-friendly areas that will make better garden spaces than lawns.

Shaped lawns look like "area rugs" and help to define inviting outdoor rooms. Lawn oval, rectangular lawn, long skinny bowling green, doughnut with a central planting bed . . . these are just a few of the possibilities. Cul-de-sacs or keyhole beds will give you the most planting space and the least lawn. You could use a low groundcover or low and slow lawn grasses instead of traditional turfgrasses for an equally inviting, lower maintenance, and more eco-friendly alternative.

If you want to keep your lawn plants out of your garden areas, a good barrier will save you a lot of weeding. Alternatively, you can make a softer transition between garden spaces by choosing lawn plants that double as an understory for adjacent planted areas; then you will not have to work to keep them separate.

watering

- Plant lawn grasses that fit your area's climate and your site's soil and geography, or use well-adapted groundcovers instead of grasses.

- If you have a lawn that needs more water than your climate supplies, boost the rainwater it gets. Shape the lawn as a shallow, flat basin that will naturally collect runoff from the surrounding landscape. Consider directing your roof runoff to your lawn as well.

- If your climate is hot and dry, protect your lawn from frying by surrounding it with trees (in planting beds) that cast light shade. Choose evergreens or trees with small leaves that break down easily or that can be easily chopped up with a mower and/or left on the lawn after they fall.

- If you must water your lawn to keep it alive and healthy, choose a moisture-sensing irrigation system that is smart enough to water only as needed, not on a timed daily or weekly schedule. Be sure your level of irrigation is adjusted seasonally to match your region's changing conditions.

- If your lawn wants to go dormant during dry periods, let it.

fertilizing

- Choose lawn plants that are adapted to your site's existing soil fertility. A low-fertility site left unamended is less prone to weed invasion and more easily dominated by well-adapted plants. For a high-fertility site, choose plants that can use the abundant nutrients and crowd out competitors.

- If you mow your lawn, leave the clippings on it unless it is planted with species that prefer low fertility. Mow over light layers of fallen leaves to give it a nutritious natural feeding that will help lawn grasses green up earlier the next spring.

- If your lawn species prefer higher fertility, plant nitrogen fixers like white clover in your lawn to naturally fertilize it. In sites where it is well adapted, clover alone makes a long-lasting, low-care lawn.

- Refrain from using chemical fertilizers and pesticides, which reduce soil life. Having a healthy soil life will increase aeration (worms and other channelers) and nutrient availability (decomposers), and will help your soil hold more water too. These soil organisms will do the work of creating rich, well-aerated soil for you, for free, if you keep your lawn chemical-free.

- For extra fertility (slow-release, so more of it will be used by your plants), apply a topdressing of compost, alfalfa meal, or other non-synthetic, slow-acting fertilizer annually. Timing depends on your lawn species.

mowing and seeding

- For safer mowing, use more level areas as lawns.

- For the least mowing, choose species that grow slowly or stay low.

- Use an electric or push mower to reduce your contribution to local air and noise pollution and your fossil fuel consumption. For edging, an electric weed whip, cordless or with cord, is lightweight, quiet, and much quicker than hand clippers; it's not prone to the engine problems of a gas weed whip, and cleaner too.

- Mow no lower than the recommended height for the dominant grass in your lawn; usually this is no lower than 3 inches.

- Take off no more than one-third of the blades at one mowing.

- Don't mow in dry periods or when the lawn is stressed.

- Some low and slow grasses will be encouraged to grow thicker (producing more sideways shoots) if you mow them annually.

- To keep grasses thick and healthy and help them resist weeds, overseed in the fall. (Or let them grow to maturity and produce seeds, and they will take care of this job for you.)

For the most up-to-date recommendations about best practices for eco-friendly lawn care, visit the Lawn Reform Coalition website at lawnreform.org.

A no-mow strip of buffalograss (Bouteloua dactyloides) is allowed to mingle
with a xeric cottage garden,
softening the transition
between them.

part three
choice ground-layer plants

This final section highlights only a small sample of commonly available ground-layer plants, just enough to whet your interest and give you a glimpse of the countless possibilities for your landscape. Each chapter provides an alphabetical listing of choice genera or species suitable for the ground layer of a landscape. The ground layer can be less than an inch high, or it can be 4 feet high or more. It can include shrubs, ferns, grasses, mosses, or all the above.

The plants are presented in groups according to their habit of growth, to help you decide how to use them in your garden, what type of maintenance they might need, and which companions would suit them. Many are grown in one or more of the gardens featured in this book (check the index to see exactly where). Plant descriptions include scientific name, common name(s), winter hardiness zone range, origin, physical description, and information on behavior and cultivation preferences.

Self-sowing mingler johnny jump-up (Viola tricolor) creates a magical effect as an understory among bearded iris.

We gardeners have a wealth of plants available to us, enough diversity of plants to satisfy any gardener and any site conditions. For more complete plant listings, consult "Recommended References." Additionally, to choose plants that will fit well in your garden, you can turn to the following reliable sources of advice and information:

- Your state or provincial native plant society and department of natural resources will help you to identify regionally adapted plants and trusted plant growers, landscape designers, and landscape maintenance services. Native plant societies may host programs or field trips that you can attend to learn more about your region's natural areas and meet helpful, knowledgeable people who can guide you in making a regionally adapted garden.

- Some plant nurseries produce extremely helpful catalogs, with planting information and even some maintenance pointers, as well as clear and complete descriptions of the plants. Specialty catalogs can be invaluable for supplementing offerings from your local growers, who may or may not be selling plants that are well adapted to your region and your garden. Trusted specialty nurseries with helpful catalogs include High Country Gardens (for dryland plants), Prairie Nursery and Prairie Moon Nursery (for prairie plants), and Richters Herbs (for edible and medicinal plants). All can be found online.

- Other gardeners and their gardens are a rich source of ideas and support. Seek out your local garden tours and clubs, investigate the open gardens program operated by the Garden Conservancy, attend a meeting or program offered by master gardeners or other specialized groups that share your interests. Wild Ones has a national website with articles to help gardeners, and many university extension offices also have instructive websites. Landscapeforlife.org offers general information on sustainable landscaping to home gardeners.

- Visit public gardens. Botanical gardens around the country have been developing demonstration gardens to help homeowners make beautiful landscapes in all kinds of challenging conditions. You will get ideas for drought-tolerant plantings, myriad groundcovers, child-friendly landscaping, alternative turfgrass species, and edible gardens, among others. Learn from their expertise and experience. It's also helpful to look for plants that have grown to their full size in these gardens, so you will be able to anticipate what your own plants might look like five, ten, or 50 years from now and choose and site them accordingly.

- If you are interested in your region's native flora and fauna and the natural landscapes of your surroundings, you can pick up a field guide to learn much more about the natural history and natural plant communities where you live. This can be helpful as you compile your own community of plants or try to attract animals that prefer a certain community.

mounding plants

mounding plants form a sparse to dense ground-layer clump of foliage that gets broader over time. They do not travel to new areas vegetatively, though they may self-sow or create offsets (small plantlets connected to the main plant by an aboveground tether).

They can be used as living edgers that will stay put and not infiltrate the planting beds, or as low hedges to separate garden rooms. In these cases be sure to choose mounding plants whose foliage will remain attractive throughout the growing season as it will be prominently displayed.

Mounding plants can also be planted as islands in a sea of lower fill-in or mat-forming plants. Colorful or dense mounding plants can anchor a corner or the end of a border. They can be paired to mark each side of a threshold. A drift of mounding plants can be used to fill a planting area, but you need to space them just right to cover the ground. If they have bare ground between them, use a lower plant to fill in around them.

Mounding plants that self-sow may colonize an area densely enough to keep out other plants. However, it is more likely they will leave gaps that other plants can fill. Taller plants with sparse basal foliage and single stems make good companions as long as they don't cast too much shade for the mounding plants.

Agave attenuata
(century plant, foxtail agave, swan's neck agave)

Zones 10 and 11, Mexico

Description: Lacks spines. Pliable leaves 6 inches wide and 2 feet long form a rosette that may reach 4 feet wide on a stout stem up to 4 feet tall. Foliage varies from pale gray-blue to pale yellow-green, depending on cultivar. Flowers are pale greenish yellow and are followed by seedpods with bulbils. *A. parryi* is similar in form but has spines and is hardy to zone 5.

Behavior: Mature plants (ten years or older) send up a 5- to 10-foot vertical flowerstalk. After flowering, the main plant dies and the bulbils grow into new plants. Snails eat foliage.

Preferences: Full sun to light shade, regular moisture. Tolerates seaside conditions. Leaf damage occurs at temperatures below 25°F. To protect from freezing, plant under a tree or overhang, or cover temporarily in freezing weather.

Aruncus aethusifolius
(dwarf goatsbeard)

Zones 4 to 8, Korea

Description: Lacy, dark green leaves form a mound 10 to 16 inches tall and wide. In late spring, feathery flowers of creamy white rise several inches above the foliage.

Behavior: Slowly expanding mound.

Preferences: Evenly moist, rich soils in part to full shade. Foliage declines if soil dries out.

Astilbe ×arendsii
(false spirea)

Zones 4 to 8, hybrid

Description: Clumps of fern-like leaves grow 18 to 24 inches tall. Slender, erect stems rise 2 to 3 feet holding plumes of flowers in shades of cream, pink, purple, or red, depending on the cultivar. Dried seedheads remain intact for months, adding winter interest.

Behavior: Deer resistant. May self-sow.

Preferences: Moist to wet, fertile soils and part to full shade. Needs consistently moist soil in full sun. Foliage will crisp in dry soil. Salt-tolerant.

Brunnera macrophylla
(Siberian bugloss)

Zones 3 to 8, Europe

Description: Mound of heart-shaped leaves grows 12 to 18 inches high and 18 to 24 inches wide. Branched racemes of blue flowers appear in late spring and early summer. 'Jack Frost' leaves are frosty silver with green edges and green veins like cracked porcelain.

Behavior: Self-sows where happy. Brightens up a shady area.

Preferences: Shade (especially in the South) or part shade, and moist but well-drained soil. Drought or intense sun will scorch the leaves.

Carex crinita
(fringed sedge, caterpillar sedge)

Zones 3 to 9, eastern North America

Description: Strap-like, fountaining, bright green leaves form dense clumps 3 to 4 feet tall. Pendent, catkin-like, showy 3-inch-long flowerspikes are yellow in late spring, turning to tan seedheads in late summer.

Behavior: Large clump-forming plant. Seeds eaten by songbirds, shorebirds, and waterbirds. Grows taller in shady and moist sites.

Preferences: Consistent moisture, sun to shade. Can handle waterlogged soil.

Cyrtomium falcatum
(Japanese holly fern)

Zones 6 to 10, Japan

Description: Glossy dark green mound of sharply serrated leaves, on arching stems, 2 feet high by 3 feet wide, makes a strong, sculptural form.

Behavior: Evergreen in frost-free climates.

Preferences: Well-drained, moist, rich, acidic soil and part to full shade. Can be cut back and divided but avoid damaging the crown.

Deutzia gracilis
(deutzia)

Zones 5 to 8, Japan

Description: Fine-textured foliage on arching, mounding shrub, to 3 feet tall by 4 feet wide. Lance-shaped leaves turn yellow or orange in fall. Showy, fragrant white flowers in spring.

Behavior: Slow grower. Dense branches create a strong structure even in winter when leaves have fallen.

Preferences: Full sun to part shade, moist well-drained soil. Can tolerate poor soil and occasional drought. Twig tips prone to winter dieback.

Echinacea purpurea
(purple coneflower)

Zones 3 to 9, eastern North America

Description: Forms a cluster of single stems to 3 feet high and wide; arranged along each stem are rough,

Several closely spaced deutzias (D. gracilis) hold the slope against weeds along a stone staircase, paired with the similar form of Japanese forest grass (Hakonechloa macra), at left.

downward-arching, dark green leaves. Single blooms 3 inches across with purple rays and orange centers appear from midsummer to fall.

Behavior: Attracts butterflies. Self-sows; seedlings of cultivars may not resemble parent plant.

Preferences: Full sun to light shade and dry soil; very drought-tolerant once established. Does not like wet soil.

Echinocactus grusonii
(golden barrel cactus)

Zones 9 to 12, Mexico

Description: Round, deeply ribbed succulent growing slowly to 24 inches high and 30 inches wide. Ribs are studded with sharp gold spines. Yellow 1- to 2-inch flowers appear on woolly flat top of barrel in early spring.

Behavior: Slow grower. Mature plants are hardier and may form offsets, becoming dense clusters. Tends to lean toward the south. Common in cultivation, but endangered in the wild.

Preferences: Full sun (light shade in very hot climates) and perfect drainage. Cannot tolerate consistently wet soil. Drought-tolerant but appreciates some supplemental water in summer.

Eupatorium purpureum
(joe pye weed)

Zones 3 to 9, eastern North America

Description: Tall, late-blooming mounding perennial has sturdy stems that reach 5 to 7 feet high with a spread of 2 to 4 feet. Dark green lance-shaped leaves. Large domed clusters of lavender-purple flowers bloom midsummer to fall, and sculptural seedheads will persist through the winter.

Behavior: Attracts bees and butterflies.

Preferences: Full sun to part shade, consistently moist soil. Leaves scorch in dry conditions.

Hakonechloa macra
(Japanese forest grass)

Zones (4)5 to 9, Japan

Description: Fountain of bladed foliage stays a foot high and spreads to a 3-foot-wide mound. Flowers in summer with subtle, airy, occasional panicles. 'Aureola' has creamy gold leaves that flush pink-red in autumn. 'All Gold' is a more upright golden-leaved form.

Behavior: Spreads slowly. Dies to the ground in winter.

Preferences: Shade to part sun and moderate moisture. Will burn in intense sunlight or dry conditions.

Helictotrichon sempervirens
(blue oat grass)

Zones 4 to 9, Europe

Description: Spiky mound of stiff, gray-blue blades, 2 feet high and wide. Bluish brown flowers rise on 3-foot stems above the foliage in summer and develop a golden wheat color by fall.

Behavior: May self-sow if happy.

Preferences: Average to poor soil in full sun. Tolerates light shade and drought but requires good drainage. Rust may be a problem in humid climates.

Hemerocallis
(daylily)

Zones 3 to 10, China, Korea, Japan

Description: Arching, grass-like leaves form clumps 10 to 30 inches tall. Flowers are produced on a stiff stalk rising above the leaves. More than 30,000 registered cultivars with flowers, some fragrant, in all colors except true blue and pure white.

Behavior: In most cultivars, the flowers open one at a time and last only a day, but the bloom period may last weeks or months. Some are evergreen; others go dormant in winter. Daylilies have escaped cultivation in many areas and can be seen growing wild along roads and at abandoned homesteads.

Preferences: Fertile, well-drained soil, full sun to part shade, depending on the cultivar. Most prefer evenly moist soil; some thrive in heavier soils with poor drainage.

Heuchera
(coralbells)

Zones 4 to 8, North America

Description: Long list of cultivars, most grown for their colorful foliage, others for their graceful, ethereal sprays of flowers. Mounds of lobed leaves, many with colored veins, 12 to 24 inches high and wide. Foliage colors vary from green to maroon with silver, purple, or red variegation. Tiny, bell-shaped flowers, white to pink to red, bloom on thin stems that can reach 3 feet tall in late spring or early summer.

Behavior: Some cultivars attract hummingbirds and make good cut flowers.

Preferences: Most prefer fertile, evenly moist, well-drained soils in full sun to part shade. To prevent root heaving in cold winter climates, apply mulch after the ground has frozen.

Mounding plants at the woodland's edge including blooming **Heuchera villosa** *'Brownies' backed by variegated* **Hosta** *'Climax'.*

English lavender (Lavandula angustifolia) edges the walk in this front meadow garden of giant feather grass (Stipa gigantea) and New Zealand wind grass (Anemanthele lessoniana).

Hosta

(hosta, plantain lily, funkia)

Zones 3 to 8, Japan, China, Korea

Description: Over 1,000 cultivars, varying in size from 6 to 36 inches tall with a similar spread. Leaf shape ranges from oval to heart-shaped, with leaf size from an inch across to more than 2 feet long, depending on cultivar. Foliage might be smooth or furrowed in a variety of colors: green, yellow, grayish, or bluish, with cream or yellow variegations. In summer, stiff stalks grow from the mound and produce small, lily-like flowers of blue to lilac to violet to green to white. Some flowers are showy and fragrant.

Behavior: Mound of overlapping leaves broadens each year. Dormant in the winter months. Foliage is tasty to slugs, snails, and deer.

Preferences: Evenly moist, fertile soil in filtered or part shade, with protection from afternoon sun. Some varieties handle more sun than others and can endure some drought. All need annual rest period with temperatures below 40°F.

Lavandula angustifolia
(English lavender)

Zones 5 to 8, Mediterranean

Description: Semi-woody perennial with gray-green, aromatic, needle-like foliage. Fragrant, lavender-blue spikes of bloom appear above the leaves in summer. 'Munstead' is a compact, early-flowering cultivar, to 18 inches tall and wide.

Behavior: Evergreen in warmer climates. Self-sows in gravel. High nectar content attracts bees.

Preferences: Full sun and average, dry to medium, well-drained soil, especially in winter; otherwise, can suffer root rot. In areas with high humidity, use rock instead of organic mulch. In northern climates, provide a sheltered location and protect from winter winds.

Mirabilis multiflora
(desert four o'clock)

Zones 5 to 10, southwestern United States, Mexico

Description: Perennial mound of gray-green hairy foliage with spade-shaped leaves closely aligned along the stems, grows 18 to 24 inches high and can be 4 to 6 feet across. Bright pink, 3-inch-long, funnel-shaped, musky-scented flowers cover plants all summer long, closing during bright sun and remaining open all night.

Behavior: Dies back to the ground every winter. Pollinated by hawkmoths. Attractive to bees, hummingbirds, and quail.

Preferences: Dry, infertile soil, but can grow in any type of soil, from clay to rocky. Deep taproot makes it extremely drought-hardy. Needs hot site with full sun.

Molinia caerulea subsp. caerulea 'Variegata'
(variegated purple moor grass)

Zones 4 to 8, Eurasia

Description: Mound of foliage is 12 inches high with wide blades of variegated cream and yellow-green. In early fall, tan seedstalks with golden seedheads rise up in a fan shape 18 to 24 inches tall.

Behavior: Slow-growing mound. Foliage subsides early in winter.

Preferences: Moist, fertile, lightly acid soil and some shade in hotter climates, but can handle full sun in cooler regions. Likes cooler night temperatures.

Nepeta ×faassenii
(catmint)

Zones 4 to 8, hybrid

Description: Sprawling masses of stems grow 10 to 18 inches tall and spread to 2 feet wide. Small, furry, gray-green ovate leaves are highly aromatic. Pale lilac to deep violet-blue flowers appear along the top third of each stem, with a flush of bloom in spring continuing through summer and intermittently into fall.

Behavior: Attracts bees and butterflies. Seeds are sterile, but parent species *N. racemosa* will self-sow if happy.

Preferences: Full sun to part shade, well-drained soil. In hot summers it appreciates some protection from afternoon sun. Drought-tolerant.

Penstemon pinifolius
(pine-leaf penstemon)

Zones 4 to 10, southwestern United States

Description: Long-lived xeric native shrublet, 16 to 30 inches tall and wide, with vivid green needle-like foliage. Covered with a showy mass of tubular orange-red flowers all summer.

Behavior: Hummingbird magnet. Evergreen.

Preferences: Some afternoon shade, but grows in full sun. Appreciates but does not require some supplemental water in desert climates.

Pseudofumaria lutea
(fumewort, fumitory)

Zones 5 to 8, Europe

Description: Delicate lacy blue-green foliage grows in a foot-high mound. Yellow tubular flowers bloom just above the foliage from spring until frost.

Behavior: Self-sows with abandon unless heavily mulched; seedlings are easy to transplant but mature plants don't move well.

Preferences: Looks frail but is drought-tolerant once established and can grow in sun or shade (though happiest if protected from afternoon sun). Needs drainage in winter.

Ratibida pinnata
(grayheaded coneflower)

Zones 3 to 10, central North America

Description: Multiple leaning flower-stalks with few leaves rise 2 feet above a loose mound of basal foliage 12 to 16 inches tall and wide. Leaves near the top of each stem are lance-shaped, lower ones wider and toothed. Butter-yellow flowers with drooping petals and a prominent, dark brown central cone bloom from midsummer to fall.

Behavior: Self-sows abundantly. Tends to prefer open, disturbed sites and to become less common in densely planted areas. Attracts butterflies and bees. Foliage is a larval food for silvery checkerspot butterfly. Gold-finches eat the seeds.

Preferences: Any well-drained soil in full sun. Tolerates part shade and drought.

Rosmarinus officinalis
(rosemary)

Zones 6 to 10, Mediterranean, Spain, Portugal

Description: Upright shrub has needle-like, dark green, aromatic leaves with a prominent whitish midvein. Clear blue, tubular flowers bloom in mid spring to early summer. Can achieve a height and width of 5 feet.

Behavior: Evergreen. Culinary herb.

Preferences: Full sun and poor, well-drained sandy to clay loam soils. Drought-tolerant once established. Performs poorly in wet or heavy clay soils. In cooler climates, can be over-wintered indoors in a sunny, humid but cool room.

Sporobolus heterolepis
(prairie dropseed, northern dropseed)

Zones 3 to 9, eastern North America

Description: Clump-forming, warm season grass with arching, narrow, medium green leaves 20 inches long makes a mound 18 inches across. In the fall, the leaves turn golden with orange tints, fading to light copper in winter. In late summer, inflorescences appear on willowy stems 30 to 36 inches tall. Flowers, in shades of pink and brown, have a distinct popcorn-like aroma; they are followed by small, round seeds in autumn.

Behavior: Slow grower, and slow to establish. Grows from seed but does not freely self-sow in the garden.

Preferences: Full sun but tolerates part shade and a wide range of soils, including dry soils and heavy clays.

Stachys byzantina
(lamb's ear, woolly betony)

Zones 4 to 10, Middle East, Turkey, Iran

Description: Thick, velvety, silver or gray-green, oblong leaves form dense, knee-high mounds 1 to 2 feet wide. Spikes of small, semi-tubular, pink to purple flowers emerge in summer and rise 12 to 18 inches above the foliage. 'Silver Carpet' rarely flowers.

Behavior: Grows quickly, and spreads by self-sowing abundantly in moist ground. Attracts bees and butterflies. Edible. Slugs enjoy the foliage.

Preferences: Evenly moist, well-drained soil. Grows best in full sun in northern areas and with some afternoon shade in southern climates. Too much shade, dew, humidity, or winter moisture can lead to rot or leaf diseases.

Verbena lilacina
(lilac verbena)

Zones 7 to 10, North American West Coast

Description: Three-foot mound of deeply divided leaves is covered in fragrant purple flowers nearly year-round.

Behavior: Evergreen. Fast grower. Attracts butterflies.

Preferences: Any soil, sun to part shade. Tolerates heat and drought.

Pine-leaf penstemon (P. pinifolius) makes spectacular, long-lasting mounds of color alongside a front walk in a xeric garden.

mat-forming plants

The blue of creeping juniper (Juniperus horizontalis) mingles with golden creeping jenny (Lysimachia nummularia 'Aurea'), creeping phlox (P. subulata), and burgundy-leaved mounds of coralbells (Heuchera).

mat-forming plants cover the ground with a layer of foliage that is flat to 6 inches tall. Some form short, broadening mounds with a limited spread; others spread indefinitely by rhizomes (underground runners) or stolons (aboveground runners). They may produce flowerstalks that rise above their foliage, or their flowers may cover their foliage, or they may not flower at all. If shade-tolerant, they are good candidates for understory plantings, forming the lowest layer of a plant community and covering the ground among taller plants. If sun-loving, they can form the floor of a garden room or clearing. Some will grow well in gaps between pavers or rocks. Some can handle more foot traffic than others. To determine how well a plant might stand up to foot traffic, consider the size of its foliage (smaller leaves will recover from damage faster), the brittleness of its stems (more flexible stems can bounce back after being pressed down), and whether broken pieces will re-root, helping the plant to self-repair.

Ajuga reptans
(bugleweed)

Zones 3 to 9, Eurasia

Description: Foliage grows 2 to 4 inches high. The many available cultivars have differently shaped leaves from round to oblong, and foliage colors from light green to dark green, some tinted purple or bronze. In early spring, flowers of blue-purple, lavender, pink, or white are borne in whorls on stiff stalks that rise 6 inches above the foliage. *A. genevensis* is similar but spreads more slowly.

Behavior: Spreads indefinitely by rhizomes to form a dense, weed-resistant mat. Has escaped cultivation and naturalized in many parts of the United States and Canada. Tolerates moderate foot traffic.

Preferences: Part to full shade. Needs consistent moisture but may suffer from crown rot in humid locations or prolonged wet soil. Can grow on heavy soils.

Antennaria neglecta
(pussytoes)

Zones 3 to 8, North America

Description: Silver-green rosettes of fuzzy, spatula-shaped leaves stay less than an inch high. Flowerstalks rise up 6 to 8 inches in late spring, with pearly white hard balls of tiny flowers that become tufted seedheads.

Behavior: Spreads indefinitely by stolons to form dense mats. Allelopathic. Nectar is used by bees and butterflies. Foliage is a larval food for American painted lady butterflies. Tolerates some foot traffic.

Preferences: Part shade to full sun, moderately moist to dry soil.

Arctostaphylos uva-ursi
(bearberry)

Zones 2 to 8, North America

Description: Small, glossy, dark green oval leaves stud prostrate branches, forming a tightly woven shrub usually under 1 foot high. Some varieties stay lower than 6 inches. 'Radiant' is taller than most at about 18 inches. Light pink bell-shaped flowers in spring turn to red berries in late summer.

Behavior: Evergreen, foliage bronzes in winter. Slow grower, will spread 15 feet over many years.

Preferences: Full sun to part shade, well-drained, acidic soil.

Eriogonum umbellatum
(sulphur flower)

Zones 3 to 8, western North America

Description: Spoon-shaped gray-green leaves may be somewhat woolly and form loose, 6-inch-high mats spreading to 3 feet wide. Bright yellow to creamy white flowers are raised on candelabras or umbels several inches above the foliage in midsummer, fading to orange-brown in fall. Foliage and seedheads turn to burgundy-brown and persist through winter.

Behavior: Hard to transplant, low germination from seed. Larval host for lupine blue butterfly.

Preferences: Droughty conditions and excellent drainage, in both winter and summer. Can grow in extremely sunny, hot areas and also part shade.

Galium odoratum
(sweet woodruff)

Zones 4 to 8, Europe, northern Africa, northern Asia

Description: Aromatic plants grow 6 to 8 inches tall with lance-shaped, dark green leaves whorled around square stems. In spring, clusters of tiny, fragrant, four-petaled, white flowers top each stem.

Behavior: Spreads indefinitely by rhizomes. Can be mowed and recovers from light foot traffic. Dry winter foliage is tan-colored and retains its aroma.

Preferences: Moist, rich soil in light to full shade.

Iris cristata
(dwarf crested iris)

Zones 4 to 8, northeastern United States

Description: Dense mats of narrow, sword-shaped foliage 3 to 6 inches tall. Pale blue to lavender blooms with gold-crested falls appear in spring.

Behavior: Spreads indefinitely. Nectar source for bees and hummingbirds.

Preferences: Moist, rich soil in part to full shade. May grow in full sun with consistent moisture.

Isotoma fluviatilis
(blue star creeper)

Zones 5 to 10, Australia

Description: Foliage stays 2 inches high or lower, with tiny dark green leaves. Sky blue to dark blue flowers occur in masses in spring and summer, sporadically recurring until fall.

Sweet woodruff (Galium odoratum) blooms in spring and covers the bare legs of taller bottlebrush grass (Elymus hystrix), dampening the latter's ability to self-sow and helping lighten the gardener's workload.

Tufts of **Carex oshimensis** *'Evergold',*
a variegated sedge, appreciate their
erosion-reducing blanket of creeping
mazus (M. miquelii).

Behavior: Quick growing, indefinitely spreading. Semi-evergreen.
Overtakes lower plants; considered
invasive by some, especially in damp
areas. Walkable.

Preferences: Full sun to part shade, and
moist, well-drained soil.

Juniperus horizontalis
(creeping juniper)

Zones 3 to 9, North America

Description: Dense shrub with needled
foliage stays flat to 12 inches tall,
spreading to 10 feet or more. Foliage
is gray-green to blue; some varieties
may turn purple in winter.

Behavior: Evergreen. Some forms
spread indefinitely.

Preferences: Full sun to light shade,
well-drained soil.

Lamium maculatum
(deadnettle)

Zones 4 to 8, Eurasia

Description: Grows 6 to 10 inches
high. Oval leaves range in color from
golden to green to silver and may
be variegated. In late spring to early
summer, bunches of small, hooded
flowers emerge atop the stems.
Bloom color varies from light purple
to soft pink to white.

Behavior: Easy to grow; rambling stems take root where they touch the soil. Spreads indefinitely to form a loose mat. Recovers from light foot traffic.

Preferences: Part to full shade, and average, medium, well-drained soils.

Lysimachia nummularia
(creeping jenny, moneywort)

Zones 3 to 9, Europe

Description: Dense, leafy mat 2 to 4 inches tall. 'Aurea' has round, slightly ruffled, yellow leaves up to ¾ inch wide. In early summer, ¾-inch, cup-shaped, bright yellow flowers bloom in abundance.

Behavior: Indefinite spreader, rooting wherever leaf nodes touch the soil. Evergreen; winter foliage of the species turns burgundy. Considered invasive in parts of the United States and Canada. Tolerates moderate foot traffic.

Preferences: Full sun to part shade and moist soils. Flourishes in damp soils where other ground covers cannot grow.

Mazus miquelii
(creeping mazus)

Zones 4 to 9, Himalayas

Description: Foliage stays under 2 inches high, darker green in shade and yellow-green in sun. Lavender tubular flowers bloom at foliage level in spring and early summer. Foliage persists through winter.

Behavior: Spreads at a moderate rate to thickly cover ground. Can grow between stones and pavers. Walkable.

Preferences: Moist soil. Grows in full sun to full shade.

Phlox subulata
(creeping phlox)

Zones 3 to 8, North America

Description: Mats of needle-like leaves stay under 6 inches high and spread to 2 feet across. In spring, tubular flowers with five flat, notched, petal-like lobes completely cover plants for several weeks. Cultivars have flower colors in pink, lavender, blue, white, or pink and white stripes; some are fragrant.

Behavior: Evergreen, spreading by creeping stems.

Preferences: Sandy, well-drained soil and full sun. Tolerates hot, dry locations better than most other species of phlox.

Sedum sarmentosum
(creeping sedum)

Zones 3 to 9, Asia

Description: Sprawling stems with tiny pointed leaves form a loose mat 4 to 6 inches tall. Yellow, star-shaped, ½-inch-wide flowers bloom in late spring and early summer. Similar species include *S. acre*, with shorter leaves, and *S. linare*, with flatter leaves that aren't as fleshy. Some other low sedums are clump-forming.

Behavior: Self-sows. Spreads indefinitely by trailing stems and will naturalize over time; considered invasive in warmer areas. Cuttings of any sedum stuck in the soil will root and form new plants. Tolerates moderate foot traffic.

Preferences: Sandy to rocky soils of moderate to low fertility in full sun to light shade. Drought-tolerant. Mulch with rock; wood chips and other organic mulch may cause crown rot.

Thymus serpyllum
(creeping thyme)

Thymus pseudolanuginosus
(woolly thyme)

Zones 4 to 8, Eurasia

Description: T. serpyllum makes a mat under 3 inches tall with copious, thin stems that have overlapping small, rounded, aromatic, glossy blue-green leaves. In summer, bunches of tiny, tubular, deep pink flowers bloom. T. pseudolanuginosus is flat with tiny, oval, gray leaves that have a very mild aroma and very few minute, tubular, pale pink flowers in summer.

Behavior: Trailing stems root where they touch the soil but can grow over pavement to several feet across without rooting. Evergreen in mild winters. Flowers are frequently visited by bees. Walkable.

Preferences: Loose, sandy or rocky soils with excellent drainage and full sun. Tolerates some shade, drought, and poor, infertile soils. Will rot in wet soils. T. pseudolanuginosus benefits from winter protection.

Trachelospermum asiaticum
(Asiatic jasmine, dwarf confederate jasmine)

Zones 9 to 11, Japan, Korea

Description: Glossy, dark green, lance-shaped leaves with white veins are 1 to 2 inches long and grow thickly along trailing wiry branches. Produces creamy white, fragrant flowers in midsummer.

Behavior: Spreads at a moderate rate, forming a dense mat of foliage. Will climb trees, fences, building walls, and other structures. Evergreen. Can be cut or trimmed to keep it in bounds. Can be invasive and has naturalized in parts of the South.

Preferences: Full sun to dense shade, moderate moisture. Somewhat drought-tolerant once established. Thrives in hot, humid summers.

Trifolium repens
(white clover)

Zones 4 to 9, Eurasia

Description: Bright green, three-part leaves grow on loose stems to 3 to 4 inches tall. Round white flowers bloom all summer.

Behavior: Spreads indefinitely by stems that freely root along the ground. Easily grown from seed. Attracts bees and parasitoid wasps (an insect predator). Larval food for clouded sulfur butterfly. Nitrogen fixer. Walkable.

Preferences: Moist soils and light shade, but will grow in average, well-drained soils in full sun to part shade.

Vinca minor
(periwinkle)

Zones 4 to 9, Europe

Description: Vine with slender, woody stems and opposite, oval-shaped leaves about 2 inches long. Flowers are violet-blue, star-shaped, about an inch wide and rise above the foliage on stems 4 to 8 inches tall. Many blooms emerge in spring and intermittently through the summer. Cultivars are available with different colored flowers or variegated foliage.

Behavior: Quick growing, indefinite spreader. Stems spread along the ground, rooting at every node. Evergreen. Considered invasive in parts of the United States and Canada. Tolerates light foot traffic.

Preferences: Moist soil, but will grow in almost any soil, in shade to full sun. Needs shade in zones 8 and 9.

Low, mounding violets (purple-tinted Viola labradorica and variegated V. grypoceras var. exilis 'Sylettas') and deadnettle (Lamium maculatum) grow in the gaps among a creeping sedum's stems.

fill-in plants

fill-in plants spread densely enough to outcompete other plants, forming a single-species stand or monoculture. When planted in a mixed bed, regular and frequent intervention may be needed to control them. Quick-growing fill-in plants work best when used alone, in areas where they will be allowed to continue spreading or where their spread will be checked by a barrier or by dense shade, moist soil, or other site conditions they cannot tolerate. Slow-growing fill-in plants may be planted among other plants that will either resist being overtaken or that the gardener will eventually have to protect by keeping the slow fill-in plants cut back. These companion plants may also be used among slow fill-in plants to temporarily hold ground until they can cover it.

If shade-tolerant, fill-in plants work well to cover ground under trees and shrubs or around tall ornamental grasses and flowers. Low fill-in plants can be used in sun or shade as the understory for established taller plants, and their dense coverage may reduce or prevent self-sowing of the taller plants. This could be a way to reduce maintenance.

Indefinitely spreading fill-in plants can be held in check by periodic clipping or pulling as well as by the above-mentioned barriers. Those that self-sow can be prevented from spreading by cutting off the flowers before seed ripens.

Some fill-in plants, like Chinese astilbe (A. chinensis var. pumila), spread at a moderate rate to a limited breadth and can be counted on for long-lasting blooms as well as dense, weed-suppressing foliage.

Achillea millefolium
(yarrow, milfoil)

Zones 4 to 8, Europe, western Asia

Description: Gray-green, finely divided, aromatic leaves resembling small ferns appear early in spring. In summer, flat clusters of flowers 2 to 3 inches across grow on stiff stalks 1 to 3 feet tall. Species flowers are white or light pink; cultivar flower colors range from white to gold to pink to apricot to red. 'Moonshine' and 'Moonwalker' are yellow-flowered, mounding hybrid cultivars; the latter is fragrant.

Behavior: Spreads indefinitely by rhizomes. Likely to self-sow as well. Considered invasive by many.

Preferences: Poor, infertile soils with good drainage in full sun. Drought-tolerant once established.

Anemone canadensis
(Canada anemone)

Zones 3 to 9, North America

Description: Showy spring wildflower with deeply divided green leaves grows 1 to 2 feet tall. Saucer-shaped, 2-inch flowers, white with yellow centers, are held on stiff, short stems just above the foliage.

Behavior: Spreads indefinitely by rhizomes. Hard to remove once established. Stays low enough to spread under and among taller established plants. Stems are more intermittent in shade, making it more of a mingler there.

Preferences: Moist, rich soils in light shade to full sun.

Artemisia ludoviciana
(prairie sage)

Zones 3 to 9, west and central North America

Description: Erect stems with aromatic, furry, whitish green, narrow leaves stand 2 to 3 feet tall. Produces dense 8-inch panicles of tiny, yellowish flowers in late summer to early fall.

Behavior: Spreads by rhizomes, sending up new stems among other plants. Can be cut in fall for low rosettes of foliage through the winter.

Preferences: Good drainage and full sun to light shade. Grows straighter and shorter in poor soils. Drought-tolerant.

Astilbe chinensis var. pumila
(Chinese astilbe)

Zones 4 to 8, Siberia, China, Korea

Description: Grows 6-inch-tall clusters of compound green leaves; plumes of lilac-pink flowers are borne on stems 9 to 12 inches long in early to mid-summer.

Behavior: Unlike mound-forming *A. ×arendsii*, *A. c.* var. *pumila* spreads indefinitely by rhizomes. Dried seed-heads provide interesting form and texture.

Preferences: Moist, rich soils in part to full shade. Leaves will turn brown in dry soils and may wilt in waterlogged soils. Can tolerate more sun and drought than other astilbes.

Carex flacca
(blue sedge)

Zones 4 to 9, Europe, North Africa

Description: Blue-green grass-like foliage grows 6 to 12 inches tall and 12 inches wide. Summer flowerspikes of greenish white appear among and a few inches above the foliage. Foliage develops yellow "highlights" in fall, while seedheads turn gray-brown and persist into winter.

Behavior: Clumps gradually fill in via rhizomes to form a dense sod. Spreads quicker in moist locations. Does well under trees. Cutting it down forces lateral shoots, making it thicker. Has naturalized in parts of North America. Walkable.

Preferences: Dry to wet soils, full sun to part shade. Very drought-tolerant once established.

Carex oshimensis 'Evergold'
(Oshima kan suge)

Zones 6 to 9, Japan

Description: Cream and green variegated, slender, weeping blades make dense mops 12 to 16 inches high and wide. *C. morrowii* 'Ice Dance' looks similar but has stiffer, wider blades, prefers moist soil, and spreads slowly by rhizomes to form patches; *C. m.* 'Variegata' is also similar but clump-forming rather than spreading.

Behavior: Evergreen in the South. Withstands occasional foot traffic.

Preferences: Average to dry soil, part to full shade. Suffers in extreme heat.

Carex 'The Beatles'
(vernal sedge)

Zones 4 to 9, Europe

Description: Forms dense, 8-inch-high mopheads of narrow green blades;

foliage is dark green in shade, yellow-green in sun. Fuzzy small yellow flowerspikes appear among the leaves in early spring.

Behavior: Evergreen in mild climates. Slowly spreads by rhizomes to form a colony.

Preferences: Full sun to part shade, moist to wet soil.

Convallaria majalis
(lily-of-the-valley)

Zones 2 to 7, northern Eurasia

Description: Wide lance-shaped green-blue leaves stand upright, 10 inches high, enfolding flowerstalks that dangle tiny white, fragrant, bell-shaped flowers in early spring.

Behavior: Spreads indefinitely by rhizomes to form dense colonies.

Preferences: Part to full shade with ample moisture.

Diervilla lonicera
(diervilla, northern bush-honeysuckle)

Zones 3 to 8, eastern and midwestern North America

Description: Semi-arching, deciduous shrub 2 to 3 feet high with oblong, pointed leaves. Small funnel-shaped

yellow flowers appear in midsummer. Foliage turns orange and red in fall.

Behavior: Spreads by suckers to form thickets.

Preferences: Slightly acid soil, good drainage, and some shade. Tolerates full shade and dry and poor soils.

Epimedium
(barrenwort)

Zones 5 to 9, Asia

Description: Slightly overlapping, heart-shaped leaves on divided branches make dense mounds of foliage 12 inches tall. Young leaves can be red-tinged or have red margins. Many cultivars with different flower colors and forms; flowers emerge in late spring and are often two-toned and dangle just above the foliage. Fall foliage can be red to purple.

Behavior: Slow spreader by rhizomes. Some forms are evergreen.

Preferences: Some morning sun, and rich, moist, well-drained soil with a cool root zone. Tolerates light to full shade and, once established, drought and competition from tree roots.

Fragaria virginiana
(wild strawberry)

Zones 3 to 6, North America

Description: Foliage stands 4 to 6 inches tall with trifoliate green leaflets. Half-inch, five-petaled white flowers appear in spring, followed by small, fragrant, edible red berries. Said to be the sweetest and most delicious wild strawberry. Similar is *F. chiloensis*, which is hardy in zones 5 to 9 and prefers sandy soil and full sun.

Behavior: Spreads by rooting new plantlets produced on stolons. Larval host for grizzled skipper and gray hairstreak butterflies.

Preferences: Dry part shade.

Geranium macrorrhizum
(bigroot geranium)

Zones 4 to 8, Yugoslavia

Description: Fresh green, divided leaves make a dense, lightly aromatic blanket of foliage 12 to 16 inches high. In summer, lavender-purple flowers with protruding red stamens bloom on stiff stalks several inches above the foliage. Leaves turn purple-brown, bronze, and scarlet in fall. *G. maculatum* is similar but shorter and mounding.

Behavior: Spreads quickly by rhizomes. Semi-evergreen.

Preferences: Full sun to part shade, moderate to dry soil. Drought-tolerant once established.

Itea virginica
(Virginia sweetspire)

Zones 5 to 9, southern United States

Description: Upright, then arching shrub to 5 feet high and 10 feet wide. Creamy white, strongly fragrant 6-inch-long racemes of flowers in early summer. Showy fall color of mixed orange, yellow, and scarlet. 'Henry's Garnet' is a dwarf cultivar, 3 to 4 feet high and wide, with dark red fall foliage.

Behavior: Grows slowly, especially in northern climes. Semi-evergreen in warmer regions. Species is suckering, but 'Henry's Garnet' is not.

Preferences: Moist soil but very adaptable, tolerating sun to shade and dry to wet sites.

Lamiastrum galeobdolon
(yellow archangel)

Zones 4 to 8, Eurasia

Description: Loose blanket of foliage grows 12 inches high with ovate green leaves that have splashes of silver. Yellow flowers flecked with brown are borne in whorls around the stems in late spring.

Behavior: Spreads indefinitely by stolons and rhizomes. Can be sheared to renew foliage.

Preferences: Part to full shade and medium moisture, but can tolerate drought once established.

Liriope spicata
(creeping lilyturf)

Zones 5 to 10, China, Vietnam

Description: Coarse grass-like blades grow in clumps roughly 12 inches high. Erect spikes of white to lavender blooms appear amid the foliage in late summer and early fall, followed by black berries.

Behavior: Spreads by rhizomes to form dense colonies. Spreads more slowly in shade. Can be cut to renew foliage. Can compete under shallow-rooted trees. Evergreen in the South, but foliage turns brown in cold winters. *L. muscari* is similar but does not run; it forms 12- by 18-inch mounds and has lilac-purple flowers.

Preferences: Grows well in nearly any soil, dry to wet, in sun to shade.

Matteuccia struthiopteris
(ostrich fern)

Zones 3 to 8, Europe, eastern Asia, eastern North America

Description: Upright clumps of lacy fronds are 3 to 4 feet high. Sterile fronds emerge in spring, gradually deteriorating over the season and going dormant in winter. Central spikes of dark brown (fertile fronds) grow 2 feet high and remain year-round.

Behavior: Spreads by rhizomes, producing offsets 4 to 8 inches apart and forming dense colonies. Combines well with early spring wildflowers, which emerge and bloom before the ferns rise up and shade them out.

Preferences: Average to wet soils and part to full shade in cooler climates; does poorly in hot, humid weather.

Microbiota decussata
(Siberian cypress, Russian arborvitae)

Zones 2 to 7, Siberia

Description: Coniferous shrub 1 to 2 feet high has arching, needled branches. Foliage is mid-green in summer, purple-brown in winter.

Behavior: Evergreen. Spreads indefinitely. Makes an extremely low-care underplanting for taller trees and shrubs.

Sterile fronds of ostrich fern (Matteuccia struthiopteris) unfurl amid spring-blooming Virginia bluebells (Mertensia virginica) and mat-forming periwinkle (Vinca minor).

Year-round groundcover Siberian cypress (Microbiota decussata) sports its rusty autumn foliage.

Preferences: Good drainage, some moisture, and protection from scorching sun and hot, humid weather. Tolerates shade. Withstands wind and snow.

Monarda didyma
(bee balm)

Monarda fistulosa
(wild bergamot)

Zones 3 to 9, eastern North America

Description: Clusters of lanky 3-foot stems with oblong pointed leaves bear showy, 3-inch, lavender (in *M. fistulosa*) or red to crimson (in *M. didyma*) flowers all summer. Foliage and flowers are fragrant.

Behavior: Can self-sow. Spreads by rhizomes. Nectar attracts bees, hummingbirds, butterflies, and sphinx moths. Infrequently browsed by deer and rabbits.

Preferences: Dry to medium soil moisture and part shade to full sun. Needs good air circulation, or it will develop powdery mildew.

Ophiopogon japonicus
(mondo grass)

Zones 6 to 10, Asia

Description: Forms dark green, grass-like clumps of foliage 8 to 12 inches tall. 'Nanus' (dwarf mondo) stays 2 inches tall. Short spikes with tiny, bell-shaped, white flowers emerge in summer, followed by round, blue-black berries.

Behavior: Evergreen. Mounds gradually increase in size to create a dense, weed-resistant turf. Deep-rooted plants are hard to eradicate after they are established. Considered invasive in southern states. Tolerates some foot traffic.

Preferences: Moderate moisture, fertile soil, and protection from afternoon sun. Tolerates any soil type.

Pachysandra terminalis
(pachysandra)

Zones 5 to 9, Asia

Description: Shiny dark green scalloped leaves grow in tight whorls around fleshy, upright stems 6 to 12 inches tall. Small, fragrant white flowers bloom in early spring on 2-inch spikes above the foliage. The related Allegheny spurge (*P. procumbens*) is native to the southeastern United States and hardy in zones 6 to 8; it grows 6 inches tall, with mid-green to blue-green matte leaves in looser whorls, and it spreads much more slowly than *P. terminalis.*

Behavior: Spreads indefinitely by rhizomes to form large colonies.

Preferences: Part to full shade. Tolerates any but very dry soil. Leaf blight can occur in high humidity or with too much water. Protect from winter winds.

Polygonatum odoratum var. thunbergii 'Variegatum'
(variegated solomon's seal)

Zones 4 to 8, Eurasia

Description: Arching, dark red stems 3 feet tall have protruding wide, oval, light green leaves edged with creamy white. Delicately fragrant, bell-shaped flowers dangle from the stems in early summer, followed by dark blue round berries. Foliage turns gold in fall.

Behavior: Slowly spreads by rhizomes to form a thick colony. Slugs enjoy the foliage.

Preferences: Part to full shade, with protection from hot afternoon sun, and good drainage. Appreciates moist, fertile soil but is drought-tolerant once established.

Primula japonica
(primrose)

Zones 3 to 8, Japan

Description: Forms low, 12- to 18-inch-wide rosettes of long, broad, yellow-green, waxy leaves. Stiff stems 12 to

18 inches tall bear clusters of dark pink to white flowers in spring.

Behavior: Self-sows abundantly where happy. Ideal weed-suppressing groundcover for wet, partly shaded areas.

Preferences: Moist soil, and needs protection from sun for part of the day. Does not do well in drought or heat.

Rhus aromatica
(fragrant sumac)

Zones 3 to 9, eastern North America

Description: Trifoliate, scalloped, aromatic green leaves. Forms a shrubby thicket 3 to 9 feet high and wide. 'Gro-Low' (dwarf fragrant sumac) stays 1 to 2 feet high. Tiny yellow flowers bloom at the tips of the twigs in early spring before foliage appears, then form clusters of small red berries. Catkins form on male plants and persist through winter. In fall, the foliage turns red, crimson, and orange.

Behavior: Quick-spreading. Species spreads by suckers to form colonies. 'Gro-Low' spreads by ground-level shoots. Provides food and shelter for diverse insects, birds, and browsers.

Preferences: Good to medium drainage and full to part sun. Thrives in dry part shade.

Rudbeckia fulgida
(black-eyed susan)

Zones 4 to 9, North America

Description: Fuzzy leaves form a mound to 3 feet across, from which many stiff hairy stems grow to 3 feet tall. Covered in 3-inch, daisy-like flowers with orange-yellow petals and dark brown centers that bloom from late summer through autumn.

Behavior: Spreads by self-sowing and by forming offsets. *R. hirta* is similar but mounding (produces no offsets). Seedheads provide food for chickadees and goldfinches. Foliage is larval food for silvery checkerspot butterflies.

Preferences: Evenly moist soil in full sun to light shade. Drought-tolerant.

Tiarella cordifolia
(foamflower)

Zones 3 to 7, North America

Description: Forms low (8 to 12 inches), thick masses of lobed green leaves with deep red veins. Racemes of small white star-shaped flowers (buds are pale pink) rise several inches above the foliage on wiry stems and bloom through spring and summer. Foliage may turn red-bronze in autumn. *T. wherryi* is similar but more compact and mounding.

Behavior: Spreads vigorously by stolons to form dense colonies. Evergreen in areas with mild winters, keeping red-bronze color until spring.

Preferences: Consistently moist, rich, well-drained soil, and part to full shade, especially in hot, humid climates. Can rot in waterlogged soils, especially in winter.

Tradescantia pallida
(purple heart)

Zones 8 to 11, Mexico

Description: Succulent-stemmed, trailing plant, with pointed deep purple leaves, grows 8 to 12 inches tall. Pale pink flowers bloom all summer at the branch tips; flowers open only in the mornings.

Behavior: Spreads by trailing stems that easily root in soil. Considered invasive in southern states.

Preferences: Moist soil, but tolerates drought well. Needs protection from intense sun. Top-killed by moderate frosts.

Veronica spicata
(spiked speedwell)

Zones 3 to 8, Europe

Description: Clumping perennial with upright spikes of lance-shaped green leaves, 1 to 2 feet high and wide.

Racemes of blue, crimson, or white flowers bloom all summer.

Behavior: Fast grower, spreads by rooting stems. Attracts butterflies and bees.

Preferences: Full sun and average moisture. Tolerates light shade. Prone to root rot in poorly drained soil.

Yucca filamentosa
(yucca, adam's needle)

Zones 5 to 10, southern United States

Description: Stiff, upright, sword-shaped green leaves form a mound 2 to 3 feet across and tall. Several varieties have cream or gold stripes down their leaves. In midsummer, thick stems up to 6 feet high bear cones of white, bell-shaped flowers that remain open and fragrant all night.

Behavior: Evergreen. Spreads at a moderate rate by producing offsets. Woody flowerstalk remains standing through winter. Deep-rooted and difficult to remove once established. Edible fruits and flowers.

Preferences: Full sun and well-drained soil. Extremely heat and drought-tolerant.

minglers

minglers have several different habits or growth strategies that make them combine well with other plants. Some grow straight up without branching or arching (*Koeleria macrantha*), or just take up very little space at ground level (*Liatris aspera*), so they can grow in closely spaced mixed-species communities. Some combine this slimness or sparseness of basal foliage with a habit of running and popping up here and there (*Asclepias syriaca*), so they can spread easily into and throughout patches of other species. Still other minglers (*Callirhoe involucrata*) develop long, horizontal branches that spread across the ground or weave through the foliage of other plants without smothering them.

In natural communities, minglers such as grasses or ferns will often form a fabric through which more ornamental plants are woven. This style can be mimicked in a garden to give a naturalistic look. Incorporating a fabric of minglers will also help to fill in a planting area, covering bare ground and making it less open to incursion by unwanted plants.

Allium schoenoprasum
(chives)

Zones 3 to 9, Eurasia, North America

Description: Mildly pungent, edible leaves, 10 to 15 inches high, growing in clusters. In spring, 1-inch spherical, pink-purple flowers (also edible) appear above the foliage on thin stalks.

Behavior: Self-sows, mounds broaden via rhizomes. Attractive to pollinators. Culinary herb and vegetable.

Preferences: Full sun to dappled shade and evenly moist soil, but can tolerate periods of drought. Plants can weaken from overcrowding and too much cutting.

Asarum canadense
(wild ginger)

Zones 3 to 7, eastern North America

Description: Each stemless plant is 4 to 8 inches high and produces a pair of downy, heart-shaped leaves that hover above the ground. Ground-level brown-purple flowers are hidden by the foliage. Not related to culinary ginger, though rhizomes have a similar scent. European relative *A. europaeum* has rounder glossy leaves, creeps by rhizomes to form a dense mat, and could be considered a fill-in rather than a mingler.

Behavior: New plants are created slowly by spreading rhizomes. Larval food for pipevine swallowtail butterfly.

Preferences: Moderate moisture and dense shade, but will spread into sunnier areas once established. Fairly drought-tolerant in shade.

Asclepias speciosa
(showy milkweed)

Asclepias syriaca
(common milkweed)

Zones 3 to 8, North America

Description: Erect stems 18 to 36 inches tall have pairs of well-spaced, wide, oblong, opposite leaves, with a prominent vein down the center of each leaf. Slightly fuzzy foliage is medium green on top side and lighter green on underside. Showy balls of intensely fragrant pink flowers bloom in early summer, followed by pods that gradually dry and split in late summer to fall, releasing silky hairs with attached seeds.

Behavior: Spreads by rhizomes, pushing up new stems at 6- to 12-inch intervals. Nectar attracts bees, butterflies, hummingbird moths, and hummingbirds. Larval food for monarch butterfly.

Preferences: Moderate moisture, in open sunny or lightly shaded areas.

Athyrium niponicum var. *pictum*
(Japanese painted fern)

Zones 4 to 8, eastern Asia

Description: Arching fronds are gray-green with maroon veins. Each plant forms a low wide mound, 12 to 18 inches high and 24 to 30 inches across.

Behavior: Rhizomes spread indefinitely to form new plants, making colonies in favorable conditions.

Preferences: Part to full shade and fertile, average to wet soil. Protect from strong winds.

Begonia grandis
(hardy begonia)

Zones 6 to 9, Malaysia, China, Japan

Description: Asymmetric heart-shaped olive-green leaves with red-veined undersides form a mound 18 inches tall and wide. Slender red stems support pendent, fragrant pink flowers. Blooms until frost.

Behavior: Dies to ground in winter. Easy to propagate, will self-propagate from bulbils; new plants usually show up under the parent.

Preferences: Moist, well-drained soil and full shade, though it can tolerate some morning sun.

Bouteloua curtipendula
(sideoats grama grass)

Zones 3 to 10, southern and western North America

Description: Fine-bladed grass with flowerstalks that grow 16 to 20 inches tall. Minuscule flowers (and later, seeds) hang from one side of the stems. Foliage turns golden brown with orange or red tints in fall.

Behavior: Self-sows and is easy to grow from seed. Can be grown as a turf and regularly cut as low as 3 inches without degrading. Can take moderate foot traffic, less during dormancy. Easily outcompeted by other grasses in moist conditions. Larval food for several skippers.

Preferences: Full sun to light shade, and good drainage. Drought-tolerant.

Common milkweed (Asclepias syriaca) is a desirable mingler for a butterfly garden, sending up its delectable (to monarchs) stems through its companions, such as this purple-blue salvia (S. nemorosa 'Mainacht'), and adding a delicious fragrance when in bloom.

Bouteloua dactyloides
(buffalograss)

Zones 4 to 9, southern and western North America

Description: Fine-bladed grass 3 to 10 inches high with small, inconspicuous seedheads. Cultivated varieties vary in their ultimate height; some have been bred to stay under 6 inches. Dormant (brown) in winter and in periods of drought.

Behavior: Spreads by stolons to form a dense sod. Can be grown as a turf and regularly cut as low as 3 inches without degrading. Can take moderate foot traffic, less during dormancy. Slow to establish from seed and requires care until established; can be bought as plugs. Greens up earlier in spring than St. Augustine or bermudagrass.

Preferences: Full sun to light shade, good drainage, and low fertility. Grows in all soil types but prefers clay; it is outcompeted in fertile soils. Drought-tolerant and does poorly in wetter climates (over 25 inches of annual precipitation). Sensitive to broadleaf herbicides.

Bouteloua gracilis
(blue grama grass)

Zones 3 to 10, southern and western North America, Mexico

Description: Fine-textured bunchgrass 6 to 8 inches high. In summer, it produces flowerspikes that stick out from the stems like stiff little eyelashes. Foliage turns purplish tan in fall.

Behavior: Self-sows and is easy to grow from seed. Can be grown as a turf, though it will not form as dense a turf as buffalograss (*B. dactyloides*), with which it can be combined for a low-growing lawn. Can be regularly cut as low as 3 inches without degrading. Tolerates moderate foot traffic when actively growing, less when dormant.

Preferences: Full sun to light shade, and good drainage. Extremely drought- and heat-tolerant.

Calamagrostis canadensis
(bluejoint grass)

Zones 3 to 8, North America

Description: Sod-forming, native perennial grass 2 to 4 feet tall; flowerhead rises above foliage in a lax, tan plume. Stands up well in winter.

Behavior: Spreads by rhizomes and self-sows readily. A well-established stand can resist invasion by woody plants. Flowers profusely only in wet areas.

Preferences: Sun to part shade. Moist to wet soil, but drought-tolerant once established. Frequently grows with sedges (*Carex*). Tolerates extreme acidity, waterlogged soil, and saline soil.

Callirhoe involucrata
(winecups)

Zones 4 to 9, southern and central United States

Description: Prostrate grower, staying below 8 inches and spreading to 3 feet, with attractive, deeply lobed leaves. Bright magenta-pink, cup-shaped flowers, 2 inches across, bloom all summer.

Behavior: Long, trailing stems weave through and among other plants. Self-sows where happy. Foliage enjoyed by rabbits and deer.

Preferences: Dry to medium soil moisture and good drainage, especially in winter. Likes full sun.

Carex pensylvanica
(oak sedge, Pennsylvania sedge)

Zones 4 to 8, eastern and central North America

Description: Fine-bladed, grass-like plant with fresh, bright green foliage grows 4 to 8 inches high. Height and spread vary significantly depending on available moisture. *C. lucorum* is similar and naturally grows south of *C. pensylvanica*'s range.

Behavior: Spreads by rhizomes. Very difficult to germinate from seed; purchase plugs or plants. Greens up early. Can be mowed to remove seedheads. Mowing makes it thicker as does some watering. Can take some foot traffic. Semi-evergreen in milder climates.

Preferences: Full shade to full sun and moderate moisture, but tolerates dry soil well.

Winecups (Callirhoe involucrata) mingles without smothering or shading out lower plants.

Dryopteris erythrosora
(autumn fern)

Zones 6 to 9, Japan

Description: Fern with open, airy arched foliage 18 inches tall and 24 inches wide. New foliage is copper-red, changing to green as it matures.

Behavior: Semi-evergreen in mild climates. Slow creeper. Self-sows where happy.

Preferences: Moist, rich woodland soil. Protect from intense sunlight and winter wind.

Festuca ovina
(sheep fescue)

Zones 5 to 10, Europe

Description: Blue-green, fine-bladed foliage grows in clumps 8 to 12 inches tall. In spring, light tan flowerstalks extend a few inches above the foliage.

Many grasses weave around and through other plants, supporting them visually and sometimes physically as well. Here, an impromptu bouquet of junegrass (Koeleria macrantha), chives (Allium schoenoprasum), and prairie coreopsis (C. palmata).

Behavior: Fills in to form a sod if allowed to self-sow. When dry, will go dormant and turn gold; greens up when moister conditions return. Walkable.

Preferences: Full sun to light shade, low fertility. Extremely drought-tolerant; does not tolerate moist soils.

Gaillardia ×*grandiflora*
(blanketflower)

Zones 3 to 8, hybrid

Description: Loose, hairy, gray-green foliage spreads 1 foot across and 1 to 2 feet tall. Orange-red disk-shaped flowers 3 to 4 inches across, some with a bright gold outer band, bloom all summer and into fall. 'Kobold' foliage stays lower, 8 to 12 inches tall, with same-sized flowers.

Behavior: Self-sows even in dry conditions. Individual plants can be short-lived.

Preferences: Full sun to light shade. Drought-tolerant and does not do well in moist soils.

Gaura lindheimeri
(gaura)

Zones (5)6 to 9, southern United States, Mexico

Description: Grows 2 to 3 feet tall with small, lance-shaped leaves near ground level and many upright, densely clustered stems that bear flowers. Four-petaled, 1-inch, white or pink flowers have prominent red-tipped stamens and bloom spring to fall.

Behavior: May self-sow.

Preferences: Full sun. Very drought- and heat-tolerant. May need winter mulch in colder zones.

Koeleria macrantha
(junegrass)

Zones 4 to 9, North America, Eurasia

Description: Stiff, bright green blades form an upright bunch 12 to 16 inches high and 8 to 12 inches across. Foliage appears in early spring. Flowers are creamy yellow spikes held 6 inches above the foliage in early summer, drying to light tan seedheads that persist through summer and fall.

Behavior: Self-sows moderately where happy. Tolerates repeated low mowing and some foot traffic.

Preferences: Dry soil and full sun.

Liatris aspera
(rough blazingstar)

Zones 3 to 9, eastern North America

Description: Flat clump of dark green basal foliage 4 to 8 inches across and 2 to 4 inches tall emerges in early summer, then produces a stiff, 2- to 4-foot flowerstalk with numerous narrow, alternate leaves. Bright magenta flowers form separate clusters along the top 12 inches of the flowerstalk, blooming in late summer. Seed ripens in fall.

Behavior: Tall, narrow form relies on surrounding plants for support in moister conditions, though it may remain upright in dry sites. Nectar attracts butterflies and hummingbirds, and seeds are eaten by songbirds. Foliage is relished by deer and rabbits.

Preferences: Good drainage, full sun, and average moisture but can tolerate drought conditions. Protect from wet winter soil.

Lupinus Russell hybrids
(perennial lupine)

Zones 4 to 9, western North America

Description: Velvety green, deeply divided leaves form thick masses of foliage 12 to 24 inches tall and 12 to 20 inches wide. Woody hollow stems stand stiffly 12 to 15 inches above the foliage. In late spring, two-lipped closed flowers in colors from yellow to pink to purple stud each stem on all sides, making a 6- to 12-inch cone of bloom.

Behavior: Foliage catches water droplets. Nitrogen fixer. Nectar attracts butterflies and bees. Self-sows where happy. Toxic to humans.

Preferences: Consistent moisture, good drainage, and full sun, but appreciates shaded root zone. Can suffer crown rot in extremely heavy or highly organic soils.

Mentha spicata
(spearmint)

Zones 3 to 7, Europe

Description: Individual 1- to 2-foot-high, upright or leaning stems with opposite oval leaves create masses of strongly aromatic foliage. Whorled tufts of lavender-pink flowers appear at intervals along spikes in midsummer.

Behavior: Spreads indefinitely and quickly through rhizomes and can also root where stem tips contact the ground. Nectar attracts bees, butterflies, and other pollinators. Edible and makes tasty tea. Evergreen in warmer areas. Can tolerate foot traffic.

Preferences: Cool, moist, partly shaded sites. Does not tolerate dry conditions. Can survive in deep shade. Will green up earlier and last longer into fall with protection from wind. May need winter mulch in cold zones.

Nassella tenuissima
(Mexican feather grass)

Zones 7 to 10, New Mexico, Texas, Mexico

Description: Dense, erect clumps 1 to 2 feet high with delicate, hair-like blades of silvery green produce long, silky flowerstalks from spring to fall.

Behavior: Self-sows abundantly and may invade natural areas.

Preferences: Full sun to part shade, excellent drainage, and light soils. Drought-tolerant.

Phlox paniculata
(garden phlox)

Zones 4 to 8, eastern North America

Description: Stems with mid-green, lance-shaped leaves grow 3 to 4 feet tall during spring and summer. In midsummer, stems are topped by 6- to 8-inch, rounded clusters of funnel-shaped, sweetly fragrant flowers in colors from pale pink to magenta, lavender, or white; some are two-toned.

Behavior: Self-sows moderately. Nectar attracts bees, butterflies, and hummingbirds.

Preferences: Consistent soil moisture and part to dense shade. Needs protection from hot afternoon sun. Can develop powdery mildew in humid conditions. May survive in cooler areas of zone 9.

Rudbeckia triloba
(brown-eyed susan)

Zones 3 to 10, North America

Description: Branched stems grow to 5 feet high and 3 feet across. In summer they bear 1- to 2-inch flowers with rounded yellow petals and brown center cones.

Behavior: Biennial or short-lived perennial. Self-sows moderately where happy.

Preferences: Heavy but well-drained soil in full sun to light shade. Somewhat drought-tolerant, but prefers evenly moist soil.

Ruellia humilis
(wild petunia)

Zones 4 to 9, eastern North America

Description: Upright to leaning stems 8 to 16 inches tall with closely spaced pairs of fuzzy green oval leaves. Flowers are 1 to 2 inches across, delicately fragrant, pale to deep lavender with prominent dark red veins, with five petals encircling a central tube of nectar. Blooms late summer and sporadically through fall.

Behavior: Stems emerge from the ground at a distance, forming loose colonies or mingling through companion plants. Nectar attracts bees and hummingbirds.

Preferences: Poor, dry soil, where it will not be outcompeted by more vigorous plants. Can tolerate part shade to full sun and humid southern climates.

Schizachyrium scoparium
(little bluestem)

Zones 3 to 10, North America

Description: Green blades with silver-blue overtones make clumps 12 to 20 inches wide and 2 to 3 feet tall. Emerges slowly in spring, growing taller through summer. In late summer, the foliage turns deep red to purple-red, and flowerstalks produce fluffy white seedheads just above

Fragrant self-sower garden phlox (Phlox paniculata) fills bare ground between mounding orange daylilies (Hemerocallis fulva).

the foliage. Foliage gradually turns golden tan but remains upright during winter.

Behavior: Spreads by rhizomes to form a colony. Larval food for several skipper butterflies. Seeds are winter food for songbirds.

Preferences: Full sun, dry soil. Takes light shade. Can be overtaken by taller species in wetter conditions.

Solidago speciosa
(showy goldenrod)

Zones 3 to 10, North America

Description: Sturdy stems, often reddish and unbranched, with sparse lance-shaped green leaves, grow to 3 feet high. Cones of tiny gold flowers bloom late summer through autumn along the top 6 inches of each stem. Winter seedheads persist.

Behavior: Moderately spreading by pushing up new stems at a distance. Self-sows. Attracts many insects from

---

*An adept mingler, showy goldenrod (*Solidago speciosa*) combines scanty basal foliage with a habit of popping up amid other plants, as here through the green mounds of prairie dropseed (*Sporobolus heterolepis*).*

summer on, to eat its foliage, drink its nectar, or overwinter in stems and seedheads.

Preferences: Full to part sun, moderately moist to dry soil.

Sorghastrum nutans
(indiangrass)

Zones 2 to 9, eastern and central North America

Description: Blue-green blades form a narrow, upright clump 3 to 7 feet tall and 1 to 2 feet wide, remaining low through spring and growing taller as summer progresses. In midsummer, a flowerstalk rises in a showy golden plume with orange and yellow highlights 1 to 2 feet above the foliage. The plume changes to golden brown as the seeds ripen.

Behavior: Flowerstalks will fall over if not kept upright by tall companion plants. Dense roots make division and moving of mature plants difficult. Will self-sow modestly if conditions are right. Foliage is the larval food of at least one skipper butterfly. Seeds are eaten by upland game birds and songbirds, and plant is used as nesting material.

Preferences: Full sun to part shade. Tolerates moderately dry to moderately moist soil.

Symphyotrichum cordifolium
(heart-leaf aster)

Symphyotrichum ericoides
(heath aster)

Symphyotrichum novae-angliae
(New England aster)

Symphyotrichum puniceum
(swamp aster)

Zones 3 to 8, North America

Description: S. cordifolium grows about 18 inches tall and 12 to 24 inches wide and produces loose terminal panicles of blue-lavender flowers with yellow centers. S. ericoides has tiny leaves and produces closely packed 6-inch cones of white flowers with yellow centers along the stem tips. It grows 1 to 3 feet tall and wide. S. novae-angliae grows 2 to 6 feet tall on stiff, hairy stems, with clusters of 1-inch yellow-centered flowers of pale pink to deep purple. S. puniceum has a stout central reddish stem 2 to 4 feet tall with well-spaced, stiff branches 8 to 12 inches long that hold loose clusters of pale lavender flowers with yellow centers. All four species bloom in late summer, continuing into fall.

Behavior: S. ericoides spreads by rhizomes to form patches. S. novae-angliae self-sows prolifically. The nectar from all four asters attracts bees and provides crucial fall migration fuel for butterflies.

Preferences: S. cordifolium grows on moderately wet to moderately dry sites and prefers part shade. S. ericoides is extremely drought-tolerant and prefers dry, sunny, well-drained sites; it may not be hardy in colder zones. S. novae-angliae prefers open sites with moist to wet soil. S. puniceum requires consistent soil moisture and tolerates periodic flooding and part shade.

Viola tricolor
(johnny jump-up)

Zones 4 to 8, China

Description: Loose mounds of leaves grow 4 to 6 inches high and wide. Spreading stems bear many small tricolored flowers in shades of purple, gold, and white that may bloom all summer if protected from heat.

Behavior: Short-lived but self-sows profusely where happy. Typically treated as a bedding annual, but it can overwinter.

Preferences: Rich, moist soil. Can grow in full sun to full shade, but needs more shade in hotter climates.

recommended references

Baldwin, Debra Lee. 2007. *Designing with Succulents*. Portland, Ore.: Timber Press.

Calhoun, Scott. 2005. *Yard Full of Sun*. Tucson, Ariz.: Rio Nuevo Publishers.

Cullina, William. 2000. *The New England Wild Flower Society Guide to Growing and Propagating Wildflowers of the United States and Canada*. New York: Houghton Mifflin Harcourt.

———. 2002. *Native Trees, Shrubs, and Vines*. Boston: Houghton Mifflin.

———. 2008. *Native Ferns, Moss, and Grasses*. Boston: Houghton Mifflin.

Dannenmaier, Molly. 2008. *A Child's Garden*. Updated paperback ed. Portland, Ore.: Timber Press.

Darke, Rick. 2002. *The American Woodland Garden*. Portland, Ore.: Timber Press.

———. 2007. *The Encyclopedia of Grasses for Livable Landscapes*. Portland, Ore.: Timber Press.

Dunnett, Nigel, and Andy Clayden. 2007. *Rain Gardens*. Portland, Ore.: Timber Press.

Greenlee, John, photography by Saxon Holt. 2009. *The American Meadow Garden*. Portland, Ore.: Timber Press.

Helzer, Chris. 2009. *The Ecology and Management of Prairies in the Central United States*. Iowa City: University of Iowa Press.

Hemenway, Toby. 2000. *Gaia's Garden*. White River Junction, Vt.: Chelsea Green Publishing.

Hightshoe, Gary. 1987. *Native Trees, Shrubs, and Vines for Urban and Rural America*. Hoboken, N.J.: John Wiley and Sons.

Lancaster, Brad. 2008. *Rainwater Harvesting for Drylands and Beyond*. 2 vols. Tucson, Ariz.: Rainsource Press.

Lowenfels, Jeff, and Wayne Lewis. 2010. *Teaming with Microbes*. Rev. ed. Portland, Ore.: Timber Press.

Moore, Robin C., and Clare Cooper Marcus. 2008. "Healthy Planet, Healthy Children: Designing Nature into the Daily Spaces of Childhood." In Stephen R. Kellert, Judith H. Heerwagen, and Martin L. Mador, eds. *Biophilic Design*. Hoboken, N.J.: John Wiley and Sons. 153–204.

Ogden, Scott, and Lauren Springer Ogden. 2008. *Plant-Driven Design*. Portland, Ore.: Timber Press.

Pollan, Michael. 2009. *Food Rules*. New York: Penguin.

Roth, Sally. 2006. *Bird-by-Bird Gardening*. Emmaus, Pa.: Rodale.

Shaw, Daniel, and Rusty Schmidt. 2003. *Plants for Stormwater Design*. Saint Paul: Minnesota Pollution Control Agency.

Shepard, Lansing, and Paula Westmoreland. 2011. *This Perennial Land*. Minneapolis: Perennial Lands.

Stein, Sara. 1997. *Planting Noah's Garden*. Boston: Houghton Mifflin.

Steiner, Lynn. 2010. *Prairie-Style Gardens*. Portland, Ore.: Timber Press.

Stibolt, Ginny. 2009. *Sustainable Gardening for Florida*. Gainesville: University Press of Florida.

Tallamy, Douglas W. 2009. *Bringing Nature Home*. Updated and expanded ed. Portland, Ore.: Timber Press.

Tatroe, Marcia, photography by Charles Mann. 2007. *Cutting Edge Gardening in the Intermountain West*. Boulder, Colo.: Johnson Books.

Tukey, Paul. 2007. *The Organic Lawn Care Manual*. North Adams, Mass.: Storey Publishing.

Wasowski, Sally, photography by Andy Wasowski. 2002. *Gardening with Prairie Plants*. Minneapolis: University of Minnesota Press.

useful conversions

inches	centimeters
¼	0.6
½	1.25
¾	1.9
1	2.5
1¼	3.1
1½	3.8
1¾	4.4
2	5.0
3	7.5
4	10
5	12.5
6	15
7	18
8	20
9	23
10	25
12	30
15	38
18	45
20	50
24	60
30	75
32	80
36	90

feet	meters
1	0.3
1½	0.5
2	0.6
2½	0.8
3	0.9
4	1.2
5	1.5
6	1.8
7	2.1
8	2.4
9	2.7
10	3.0
12	3.6
15	4.5
18	5.4
20	6.0
25	7.5

temperatures

$$°C = 5/9 \times (°F{-}32)$$
$$°F = (9/5 \times °C) + 32$$

photo locations and credits

Photography by the author except where noted.

Cover, pages 6, 31 (except top left), 33 top, 40, Susan Harris Garden, Takoma Park, Md.
Photos: Saxon Holt.

Frontispiece, pages 16, 141 top, 142, 175 bottom, Mayberg Garden, Edina, Minn.
Design: Erik James Olsen / Out Back Nursery. Photos: Saxon Holt.

Pages 8, 15, 31 top left, 50–51, 63, 66, 160–162, 177, 199, Olbrich Botanical Gardens,
Madison, Wisc. Photos pages 15, 66: Jeff Epping.

Pages 12, 43–44, 172, 181–182, Kalantari Garden, Richfield, Minn. Design: Paula
Westmoreland / Ecological Gardens.

Pages 19, 35, 56, 80, 82, 88–89, 119–120, 153, 200, California. Designs pages 19,
80, 88: Michael Thilgen / Four Dimensions Landscape. Design page 82: Sonny
Garcia. Designs pages 119 top, 200: Maile Arnold. Design page 119 bottom: Patrick
Anderson. Design page 153: Robyn Sherrill. Photos: Saxon Holt.

Pages 20, 28, 54, 64, 96 bottom, 139, 211–212, Holman Garden, Stillwater, Minn.
Design: Diane Hilscher / Hilscher Design and Ecology. Photos pages 20, 28, 54, 64,
139: Saxon Holt. Photo page 96 bottom: Diane Hilscher.

Pages 23, 124, 127 top, 168–169, Rosalind Creasy Garden, Los Altos, Calif. Photos:
Saxon Holt.

Pages 24 top, 37 top, Beaufort, S.C.

Pages 24 bottom, 134–135, Delano, Minn.

Pages 26–27, 68, 71–72, 131 top, 218 top, Smith Garden, Maplewood, Minn. Design:
Paula Westmoreland / Ecological Gardens.

Pages 33 bottom, 34, 175 top, Hult Garden, Plymouth, Minn. Photos: Saxon Holt.

Pages 37 bottom, 38 top, 156–157, 218 bottom, Minnesota Landscape Arboretum, Chaska.

Page 38 bottom, Fleming Garden, Berkeley, Calif. Photo: Saxon Holt.

Pages 39, 48–49, 53 bottom, 70, 83–84, 94, 96, 99–100, 133, 141 bottom, 154, 165, 178, 190–191, 204, 207, 225, 227, 240, Minneapolis / Saint Paul metro area. Designs pages 48, 70: Paula Westmoreland / Ecological Gardens. Designs and photos page 96: Diane Hilscher. Photo page 99: Michael Schumacher. Photo page 100 left: Lindsay Rebhan.

Pages 42, 208, Mary Livingston Ripley Garden, Smithsonian Institution, Washington, D.C.

Pages 46–47, Sifford Garden, Charlotte, N.C.

Page 53 top, West of the Lake Gardens, Manitowoc, Wisc.

Pages 57–58, 221, Haigh-Canon Garden, Golden Valley, Minn. Photos pages 57 top, 58 top: Saxon Holt.

Pages 61–62, 185, 215, 222, 228, Damon Garden, Saint Paul, Minn.

Page 67, Saint Louis, Mo. Design: Matt Moynihan. Photo: Saxon Holt.

Pages 73–74, Gupta Garden, Minnetonka, Minn. Design: Paula Westmoreland / Ecological Gardens.

Pages 76–77, 232, University of Wisconsin-Madison Arboretum.

Pages 79, 150–151, 193, 218, Willenberg Garden, Plymouth, Minn. Design: Diane Hilscher / Hilscher Design and Ecology.

Pages 85–86, 252, Kostroski-Polucha Garden, Hugo, Minn.

Page 87, Pittsburgh, Pa.

Page 90 top, Becker Garden, Garden City, Idaho.

Page 90 bottom, Dinsmore Garden, Washington, D.C. Design: Marty Hays / Design InSite. Photo: Lucy Dinsmore.

Page 92, Neff Garden, Novato, Calif. Photo: Saxon Holt.

Pages 95 top, 106 bottom right, 108–109, Zieke-Lee Garden, Decorah, Iowa. Design: Lee Zieke and Lindsay Lee / Willowglen Nursery.

Pages 95 bottom, 114, 116, 121, Boise, Idaho. Photo page 116 top: Kelly Broich.

Pages 97, 101, Children's Garden at Lewis Ginter Botanical Garden, Richmond, Va.

Page 98, Hershey Children's Garden at Cleveland Botanical Garden, Cleveland, Ohio.

Page 102, Maryland. Design: Oehme, van Sweden and Associates. Photo: Saxon Holt.

Pages 104–105 top, LaTourrette Garden, Los Altos, Calif. Photo: Saxon Holt.

Pages 104–105 bottom, 148, New Mexico. Design: Judith Phillips. Photos: Saxon Holt.

Pages 106 (except bottom right), 236, Weidema Garden, Brooklyn Park, Minn. Photo page 106 top right: Lisa Weidema.

Pages 111, 129–130, 194, Detwiler Garden, Concord, Calif. Design: Kelly Marshall / Kelly Marshall Garden Design. Photos: Saxon Holt.

Pages 112, 117, 203, Santa Fe, N.M. Design: Donna Bone / Design With Nature. Photos: Saxon Holt.

Page 115, California. Design and photos: Billy Goodnick.

Page 123, Ogden Garden, Colorado. Design: Lauren Springer Ogden and Scott Ogden. Photos: Saxon Holt.

Pages 127 bottom, 128, 131 bottom, Westmoreland Garden, Minneapolis, Minn. Photos pages 127 bottom, 128 center, and 131 bottom: Saxon Holt.

Page 136, Sally Robertson Garden, Bolinas, Calif. Photo: Saxon Holt.

Page 138, Lindie Wilson Garden, Charlotte, N.C.

Pages 143–145, 231, Buss Garden, Saint Paul, Minn.

Pages 146–147, Stevens Garden, Charlotte, N.C.

Pages 152, 186, 197, Washington, D.C. area.

Pages 155, 159, Graham Garden, Plymouth, Minn.

Page 158, DeBolt-Rosentreter Garden, Boise, Idaho.

Page 189, Denver, Colo. Design: Tom Peace. Photo: Saxon Holt.

index

about the author

Evelyn J. Hadden writes and speaks about lawn alternatives from coast to coast, spreading the word about eco-friendly gardening strategies, better-adapted lawns, and ways to convert turf to more satisfying landscapes. She has authored two books, including the award-winning *Shrink Your Lawn: Design Ideas for Any Landscape*, founded the website LessLawn.com, and is a founding member of the Lawn Reform Coalition (lawnreform.org).